THE STORY PERFORMANCE HANDBOOK

THE STORY PERFORMANCE HANDBOOK

R. Craig Roney
Wayne State University

LEA LAWRENCE ERLBAUM ASSOCIATES, PUBLISHERS
2001   Mahwah, New Jersey   London

Copyright © 2001 by Lawrence Erlbaum Associates, Inc.

All rights reserved. No part of this book may be reproduced in any form, by photostat, microfilm, retrieval system, or any other means, without the prior written permission of the publisher.

Lawrence Erlbaum Associates, Inc., Publishers
10 Industrial Avenue
Mahwah, New Jersey 07430-2262

Cover design by Kathryn Houghtaling Lacey

Library of Congress Cataloging-in-Publication Data

Roney R. Craig
   The story performance handbook / by R. Craig Roney.

         p.   cm.
      Includes bibliographical references and index.
      ISBN 0-8058-3628-4 (pbk. : alk. paper)
      1. Storytelling—Handbooks, manuals, etc. 2. Activity programs in education—Handbooks, manuals, etc. I. Title.
LB1042 .R64 2000
808.5'43—dc21   00-034759

Books published by Lawrence Erlbaum Associates are printed on acid-free paper, and their bindings are chosen for strength and durability

Printed in the United States of America
10 9 8 7 6 5 4 3 2

Contents

I: READING ALOUD

II: TRANSITION TO STORYTELLING

III: STORYTELLING

IV: DEVELOPING STORY PERFORMANCE PROGRAMS

Credits

Preface

In the spring of 1977 when I first arrived at Wayne State University and met Don Bissett, the senior faculty member of the Children's Literature Center to which I would be assigned, his first words to me were: "Get ready to teach the storytelling course. It will be offered in the fall." I'd never told a story formally before then and, with only a few months to prepare myself, you can imagine my feelings at the prospect of teaching this course. Aside from the anxiety of assuming the role of professor of a *performance* course (unlike the academic courses I'd previously taught), I experienced a much more basic emotion—the fear of telling a story to an audience of adults. Today, although I can now confidently deliver stories to a wide variety of audiences, including adults, I have not forgotten that initial anxiety and have come to recognize it as the single most serious impediment for adult beginning storytellers.

Needless to say, in the intervening years since I taught that first storytelling class and thanks to the patience and understanding of the many graduate students who have enrolled in the course, I've learned a great deal about storytelling, in particular, techniques for helping adults develop basic storytelling competence and confidence. From a very subjective perspective, I believe the techniques I've used in the course have been effective. I'm satisfied that my current students emerge from the course as successful beginning storytellers. I have, however, begun to subject specific teaching/learning theory and technique to empirical examination and have designed additional experimentation for the years to come. Thus, the learning will continue in a more objective and rigorous fashion. I believe, however, that the time has come to share with others what I have learned about beginning storytelling instruction based both on personal experience and the research completed to date.

The purpose of this text, then, is to provide you as adults with a straightforward sequence of progressive learning experiences that will enable you to develop basic skill in reading aloud, and storytelling while experiencing growth in confidence at every step of the way.

HOW TO ENGAGE THE TEXT

The learning experiences in the text are ordered sequentially, and it is recommended that you follow the sequence from one chapter to the next. Reading aloud, like storytelling, is an art form and is of value in its own right as an enjoyable and relatively convenient form of story communication. However, it also serves as a confidence builder and natural lead-in to the more challenging art of storytelling. This is because adults frequently have had more experience with reading aloud than with storytelling. As such, many of you will be working from the known to the unknown as you progress through the text. In addition, following the chapters in sequence is recommended because the progression through the chapters involves a gradual reduction in reliance on plot reminders (the printed text in reading aloud and manipulatives like feltboard pieces in mediated storytelling).

Beside this progression from an easy to more difficult form of story delivery, there are two other sequential patterns that undergird the text. As you move from one chapter to the next, you are required, of necessity, to prepare for story delivery in greater and greater depth, thus reinforcing the critical notion that the key to successful story performance is the quality of the preparation prior to performance. In turn, this progression enables you to develop a more finely tuned sense of the narrative structure that serves as the basis for your imposing narrative structure on anecdotal material in creating your own original stories.

Although it is recommended that you follow the text in sequence, the point at which you enter the sequence depends on your experience with the various types of story presentation exposed in each chapter. Someone experienced and confident in reading aloud from all types of printed material, for example, could begin with chapter 6, launching immediately into storytelling skill development.

CHAPTER OVERVIEW

Chapter 1, Introduction to Reading Aloud, establishes the value of reading aloud, particularly with regard to children's academic growth, and provides the basis for viewing it as an art form. In chapter 2, Reading Aloud Picture

Books, you learn how to select, prepare, and deliver picture book stories including texts in *big book* format. In chapter 3, Reading Aloud Chapter Books, you are introduced to similar techniques for texts with few or no pictures. Special techniques for reading verse text are provided in chapter 4, Reading Poetry Aloud. Chapter 5, Sharing Stories Through the Use of Props, serves as a transition chapter from reading aloud to storytelling. Here you learn to perform stories with wordless picture books and props such as the felt board and the overhead projector. Chapter 6, Introduction to Storytelling, extends the theoretical perspective introduced in chapter 1 to include the art of storytelling. In this chapter, a definition and a model of storytelling are provided, and a distinction is drawn between storytelling and reading aloud. In chapter 7, Stand-up Storytelling, you discover specific techniques for selecting, preparing, and delivering stories specifically geared to the beginning teller as well as information regarding the ethics of telling stories created by other storytellers. Techniques for developing your own stories for telling are provided in chapter 8, Telling Your Own Self-Created Tales. Chapter 9, Creating a Story Performance Program, introduces you to strategies for putting together story performance programs for general use and storytelling lesson and unit plans for use in schools and school libraries.

PEDAGOGICAL FEATURES

The text includes several special features. Samples of children's and adolescent literature are cited throughout the text to augment the presentation of specific concepts exposed in various chapters. Special processes related to preparing for a story performance have been indented and placed in bold type. These processes include:

- Questions to ask in looking at the format of a book and judging its appropriateness for children of varying ages.
- Directions for identifying themes in stories.
- Questions to ask in selecting picture books to read aloud to larger audiences.
- Questions to ask in analyzing the illustrations for a reading aloud performance.
- Questions to ask in analyzing the text for a reading aloud performance.
- Questions to ask about yourself before a reading aloud performance.

Multiple figures provide specific additional information; they have been numbered sequentially within each chapter and are located in boxes for easy access. These figures include:

- Forms for preparing for reading aloud picture books and chapter books, and for storytelling stories in original print format and self-created stories.
- Symbols used in making performance notes in a chapter book to be read aloud.
- Drawings of characters for overhead projector stories.
- A model of the storytelling process.
- A model of narrative structure.
- A list of common story motifs.

Moreover, specific skills are exemplified throughout the chapters. These examples are numbered sequentially within each chapter and are highlighted with background shading to facilitate their location. They include:

- Theme identification for two stories.
- Plot-Concept, Theme-Trait matching process for three stories.
- Descriptions of picture book hand-holding positions.
- Samples of good and bad text created for a wordless picture book.
- Storytelling preparation notes for two felt board stories, an overhead projector story, a story from a book, and a self-constructed story.
- Analysis of the narrative structure of a story.
- List of personal anecdotes generated from a generic list of story motifs.
- Sample story performance programs for children and adults.
- Sample lesson and unit plans employing story performance in the school curriculum.

In addition, the end of each performance chapter features lists of developmental and culminating activities that help improve your reading aloud and storytelling skills, as well as lists of additional resources to augment your knowledge of story performance.

INTENDED AUDIENCE

The intended audience for the text is any adult interested in developing basic skill in delivering stories to an audience through reading aloud and storytelling. It is not intended as a text for developing the professional (or freelance) teller, although it may be that some of you who master basic skill via the text could eventually develop a professional level of expertise. This text is most valuable to teachers, librarians, clergy, parents, and the like who find reading aloud and storytelling useful in carrying out the duties of these professions.

Once you've completed a first reading of the text and your experience with story performance grows, you might find it valuable from time to time to revisit specific parts of the text. The combination of your increased first-hand experience and the rereading may provide you with new insights that were not readily apparent during the first reading.

Although the text is designed to be used primarily in a college classroom or workshop setting, it can be read independently, as a self-help guide, the theoretical aspects of each chapter serving as food for thought prior to employing the theory and testing your skill via the extended practice activities. Moreover, I have discovered that most, if not all, of the learning strategies provided here work as well for children and teens, assuming adults are available to model the strategies and provide direction for these younger students.

One final word about the format of the book. Some folks may claim that following the sequence in the text is much like following a cookbook. That's okay in my mind. I've savored more than a few meals prepared directly from a recipe, and I've thoroughly enjoyed many stories read aloud or told by folks who developed their talent and prepared their stories in a sequential, logical, and prescribed fashion. Then, too, it would be foolish to claim that the prescription provided in this text is the only legitimate way for someone to develop basic story performance talent. There certainly are other techniques available (see other reading aloud and storytelling texts). However, my experience and the research completed to date suggest that this prescription is an effective strategy for those of you who want to become competent, amateur story performers in a relatively short period of time.

ACKNOWLEDGMENTS

I am deeply indebted to many people whose influence, in one way or another, has helped forge my commitment to the arts of reading aloud and storytelling. As a young child, my parents constantly modeled for me the value of developing an intense interest in both print and oral literature. Thanks to my father for being the consummate reader and especially to my mother for the thousands of precious minutes she spent reading aloud to my brother and me. Thanks too to my mother's family and especially Aunt Jane and Uncle Kate whose home in Gallitzin, Pennsylvania, served, for so many of my formative years, as center stage for all those marvelous informal family storytelling sessions.

Thanks to two very special teachers, Bro. Robert, F.S.C., for igniting my literary fire, and Virginia Westerberg, who fueled that fire by generously sharing with me her extensive knowledge of children's literature, and Mr.

Baumgartner, my college freshman composition professor, who helped me learn how to think creatively and critically through writing.

I am grateful to Don Bissett for the initial opportunity to break into story-telling and to my graduate students for their patience, understanding, and assistance in helping me perfect my talent as a story performer and instructor in the arts. Special thanks are due to John Stewig and Judith Volc for critiquing the manuscript and providing me with timely suggestions for its improvement.

I am deeply indebted to Naomi Silverman, my editor at Lawrence Erlbuam Associates, particularly for her skill in formatting this text, but more important for her enthusiasm for editing, which rivals my own enthusiasm for story performance.

Time is an essential ingredient in perfecting one's reading aloud and storytelling capability. The progress I've made as a story performer and instructor in these arts is due in large measure to the time my family has afforded me to develop my talent. For their generous gift of time, I am forever grateful.

This book is lovingly dedicated to Marlene, a natural storyteller, and to my next generation of storytellers, Nathaniel, Lara Lea, and Megan.

PART I

READING ALOUD

1

Introduction
to Reading Aloud

Reading aloud, simply defined, involves the oral sharing of some printed text where the text is in full view of the reader and, in some instances, the audience as well. Without the immediate availability of the printed text, the reader would have a difficult, if not impossible, time remembering it and sharing it effectively with the audience. The type of text is irrelevant; that is, it can be fiction, nonfiction, poetry, newsprint, or any other type of printed material. Typically, however, the art of reading aloud is commonly associated with the sharing of fiction with an audience.

THE VALUE OF READING ALOUD

The most obvious use of reading aloud is as a means of entertainment. Occasionally actors or other notable people will read stories or poetry in public performances. However, its most frequent uses are in the home, where parents read stories to young children, and in schools or libraries, where professionals share literature with students and young patrons. Aside from its entertainment value, there is much greater benefit to be derived from adults reading to children. An abundance of research over the past 40 years confirms the educational value of the practice (Galda & Cullinan, 1991; McCormick, 1977; Short, 1995, pp. 75–89, 111–116). Children who are read to frequently in the preschool years come to school with a leg up on literacy development. Initially, the benefit of listening to stories read is that it has a profound influence on their oral language development. A child's phonological range, complexity of sentence structure, and receptive and expressive vocabulary are significantly affected when children are read to on a regular basis (Burroughs, 1970; Cazden, 1965; Chomsky, 1972; Fodor, 1966; Irwin, 1960; Ninio & Bruner, 1973). Moreover, researchers have exposed a critical link between reading aloud by preschool caregivers and a child's later success in learning to read (Clark, 1976; Durkin, 1966; Sostarich, 1974; Thorndike, 1973; Wells, 1986). One researcher notes the unique impact of parents' reading aloud on the reading achievement of a child born with severe genetic disabilities (Butler, 1980).

Perhaps the reason that this link is so dramatic is because, by reading to children at an early age, adults help children develop positive attitudes toward literature and literacy. As Huck, Hepler, Hickman, and Kiefer (1997, p. 632) stated: "One of the best ways to interest children in books is to read to them frequently from the time they are first able to listen." This linkage is supported in the research (Hansen, 1969, 1973; Roney, 1975; Sirota, 1971). In addition, however, reading to children provides them with background knowledge essential in their own reading for comprehension and in the process of learning to read. By sharing literature with children through reading aloud, adults build a child's knowledge of the world, literary language, and the unique structure of a variety of types of literature, as well as the knowledge as to how the print symbol system works and the belief that reading is purposeful and enjoyable (Roney, 1980, 1984).

To understand why developing this background knowledge is so important, think of an experience you've had trying to read technical writing (e.g., a legal document, research report, textbook on astrophysics, instructions for installing an electric clothes dryer). The reason that comprehending such a document was so difficult for you was that the content, language, and/or format of the writing was outside your realm of experience. Provide you with appropriate background knowledge and you'd have little trouble comprehending the document. Children, particularly young ones who are new to the reading process, have limited experience with the world and print literature in general. Unless adults help these youngsters develop sufficient and relevant background experience with literature by reading to them in the preschool years, the likelihood is that they will have greater difficulty in school learning to read because any literature we expect them to read will be outside their realm of experience. On the positive side, the research supports the notion that adults reading to children on a regular basis significantly influences their chances of success in learning to read.

Once in school, children benefit as well from teachers and librarians reading aloud to them. Research by Cohen (1968), Cullinan (1974), and Feitelson, Kita, and Goldstein (1986) in particular has confirmed the significant influence reading aloud by teachers has on the reading achievement of primary grade children, even with children who have come to school without the essential background knowledge necessary for success in early literacy training. Although research involving children beyond the primary grades is more limited (Short, 1995, pp. 111–112), some evidence does exist that reading aloud by teachers significantly influences older as well as the younger children (Galda & Cullinan, 1991). One researcher reported significant growth in reading achievement by middle-grade children who were read to by juniors in high school (Porter, 1971).

THE ART OF READING ALOUD

Anyone with basic reading competence can read literature aloud as long as the print format is one with which the reader is familiar. However, not everyone who reads aloud can be said to be engaged in the art of reading aloud. The difference involves the amount and quality of the preparation that takes place prior to the performance. As with any art, fluency and expertise come with conscious and thoughtful practice and preparation. Just as one cannot be said to be a painter simply by mindlessly applying paint to canvas, so also one cannot be said to be an artist by picking up a book and reading it aloud with no forethought. The art of reading aloud involves the conscious and thoughtful preparation of a printed text for performance for an audience. As such, it involves developing an understanding of the elements that must be taken into consideration when selecting, preparing, and delivering literature to an audience via reading aloud.

Note that the use of the term *art* here has nothing to do with whether one becomes a professional at reading aloud. As stated in the preface, it is not my intent to develop people as professional performers (although some may choose that route later on). However, I do believe that people who use reading aloud as an integral part of their profession (be it a parent, teacher, librarian, or the like) owe it to their audiences to raise the level of their reading aloud to an art form.

2

Reading Aloud
Picture Books

Picture books rely equally on the illustrations and the print text to communicate their messages and include picture storybooks and those informational books where the pictures and text complement each other (Huck et al., 1997, p. 198). Although picture books are typically intended for young children, many are now being published that are targeted for older children and adults as well.

SELECTION

Selection of picture books to read aloud is a dual, ongoing process where the two aspects of selection are sometimes completed simultaneously. The first aspect involves developing your repertoire of literary works to be read to audiences. The second aspect involves selection of works from your repertoire for a specific performance.

For people who want to utilize their reading aloud skill exclusively with a singular type of audience, the two aspects of the selection process are usually completed simultaneously. If you are a third-grade teacher, for example, you might select and prepare a specific book to read to your class on a particular day for a specific (perhaps curricular) purpose but simultaneously add that book to your repertoire of books to read to other audiences at other times. However, others (e.g., librarians) may want to develop their talent as readers of literary works to people of a variety of ages. If you are such a person, it may happen that you would develop your repertoire of read-aloud stories independent of preparing for any specific performance, but later select from that repertoire specific stories for each performance.

Selection to Augment One's Repertoire

In either case, there are certain general guidelines that you can follow in choosing stories to augment your repertoire or to put together a read-aloud program. It is important that you choose literature that you yourself find interesting, meaningful, and enjoyable. Otherwise it is not likely that you will continue the practice of reading aloud for very long. Unless this guideline is met, your heart won't be in the preparation of the text for reading aloud, and the delivery will likely be labored or boring—fostering negative attitudes that will be communicated to your audiences. Conversely, if the literature you choose is personally valuable, you will be encouraged to share it with others and, when reading aloud, engender positive attitudes toward literature and reading—of vital concern to educators who want to motivate children to learn to read and to develop life-long reading habits.

In building your read-aloud repertoire, you will want to vary the genre of literature selected depending on your potential audiences. For example, teachers and librarians responsible for exposing children to a wide variety of literature will want to choose folk tales, fantasies, historical and contemporary realistic stories, poetry, biographies, informational texts, and the like. Religious educators, however, might limit themselves to appropriate forms of traditional tales (certainly "bible" tales, fables, myths and proverbs), but should not discount more contemporary tales such as DiSalvo-Ryan's (1991) *Uncle Willie and the Soup Kitchen* or Nones' (1995) *Angela's Wings*.

Teachers and school librarians might also want to select texts that vary in terms of their readability levels and literary quality. If the purpose of reading aloud is to motivate children to read the specific texts exposed during a program, then some easy-to-read texts (that often may not be of the highest literary quality) must be selected to accommodate children at lower reading levels. However, if the purpose is to expand a child's literary horizons, then choosing the very best in children's literature (which is often written at a high readability level) is necessary. One caution should be noted. Beware of excessive reliance on published mathematical formulas to determine the readability of texts. Whether the formulas involve simple or complicated computation, they are all invalid because they don't take into account the background knowledge or interest of the reader—the most critical elements in determining the readability of a book. You may be best off relying on your own personal judgment in this matter.

Look at the format of the book and ask yourself whether ...
-the size of the print used,
-the number of pages in the book,
-the number of words on a single page,
-the amount of blank space surrounding the words,
-the complexity of the syntax of the text, and
-the number and complexity of the illustrations ...
suggest that the text could be read by some members of your audience.

As a general rule, books for young children employ large print; few pages; few words per page; much blank space surrounding words; book language involving short and simple sentences or repeated words, phrases, or sentences; and many, simple illustrations. Conversely, books for older readers would utilize the opposite extremes of each of these elements (small print, many pages and many words per page, etc.). For example, *Rosie's Walk* (Hutchins, 1983), is intended to be read by beginning readers. The text is only 32 pages in length and is limited to 32 words (no more than 7 words per page) compressed into a single sentence. The print is quite large, with much white space surrounding the words, and each double-page spread is dominated by large, simple woodcut prints. By contrast, Polacco's (1994) *Pink and Say* could only be read by a child with more advanced reading skills. Although the book is only 48 pages long and only half the pages covered with text, there are from 50 to 200 words per page of print in sentences of varying complexity and length. Moreover, the print is relatively small with limited white space around each word.

Selection for a Specific Program

Appropriate selection of read-aloud texts for particular audiences depends primarily on creating a match between the text and the needs, interests, and capabilities of the audience members. Therefore, it is important for you to understand both the topical and thematic content of the texts you select and the developmental traits of the members of your audience.

Identifying topical content is easy enough. It simply requires reading the text then mentally listing the various topics exposed via the plot. *Rosie's Walk* (Hutchins, 1983) is a story about hens, foxes, a fox's penchant for chasing hens, various landmarks typically found on farms, and the ways in which hens might walk over, under, around, or through those landmarks. *Pink and Say* (Polacco, 1994) is about past history, war, Whites and African Americans and the interpersonal and intercultural relationships between them, survival, true friendship, injustice and prejudice, and many other concepts.

Identifying theme is typically a bit more difficult perhaps because *theme* is often confused with either *plot summary* or *motif*. Huck et al. (1997) defined *theme* as " ... the larger meanings that lie beneath the story's surface" (p. 20). In a story of any complexity, there are often several main themes that serve as its unifying elements. However, it is important to remember that these themes come in the form of complete sentences or independent clauses, as opposed to single words or phrases, and they are not simplistic plot summaries. "*Charlotte's Web* (White, 1952) is a story about a pig whose life is saved by a spider" is not a theme statement! It is a plot statement. "*Charlotte's Web* is a story about friendship" is also not a theme statement! Rather, it is a statement identifying one of the most important motifs in the story—friendship. "A theme in *Charlotte's Web* is that true friendship involves responsibilities as well as privileges" is a theme statement! Note that, in the previous sentence, the clause that specifically identifies the theme can stand alone as a complete sentence—that is, "true friendship involves responsibilities as well as privileges." In identifying themes, then, a word to be avoided is *about*. If you begin your statement this way: "This story is about ... " or "The theme of this story is about ...," it is likely that what follows will not be a theme but a plot summary or a motif. You're better off beginning this way: "A theme is that ... "

Although plot summary and motif aren't the same as theme, they can be utilized in identifying theme by following these directives.

For a chosen book:

> **First, make a brief plot summary statement using the format "This book is about.... "**
> **Second, brainstorm a list of motifs (single word or phrase concepts) about the book.**
> **Third, take one or several of the listed motifs and ask this question: What statement is the author and/or illustrator making to me about this motif (these motifs) via this book?**

The answer to this question is a theme statement. Consult Examples 2.1 and 2.2 for descriptions of the implementation of these directives with two children's books.

For people who wish to read aloud to audiences, being able to identify themes in literature is of greater value than simply as an academic exercise. In fact, theme identification is probably the most accurate way to match a

Example 2.1

Theme Identification for *Rosie's Walk*

Plot: The story is about a hen whose walk around the barnyard is undisturbed by the efforts of a fox to capture her for his supper.

Motifs: luck   minding one's own business
           determination   predictability
           obviousness   order
           just deserts   aggressiveness
           journeys   courage
           quests   security
           initiative   failing to pay attention
           reward   punishment

Themes: Good deeds are rewarded, bad deeds are punished.
           Failure to pay attention can get you into trouble.
           If you mind your own business, life will be good to you.
           Taking the initiative can be satisfying; being overly
               aggressive can lead to dissatisfaction.

Example 2.2

Theme Identification for *Pink and Say*

Plot: This Civil War story is about two teen boys, Say Curtis and Pinkus Aylee, who survive a fierce battle, become separated from their units, and, for a period of time, take refuge in the care of Pinkus' nurturing mother. Attempting to return to their units, they are captured by Confederates. Pinkus is immediately hung because he is Black while Say, who is White, is merely imprisoned.

Motifs: survival   inhumanity
           security   injustice
           courage   cultural clash
           family loyalty   friendship
           danger   fear
           discrimination   sacrifice
           love   bigotry

> Themes: Survival in an alien environment depends on the help one gets from others more familiar with the environment.
>
> A person can be both afraid and brave at one and the same time.
>
> Being a just person does not ensure that one will always be treated justly by others.
>
> Love knows no bounds.
>
> Civilians as well as soldiers suffer during wars.

text with its appropriate audience. With themes in mind, you can turn your attention to the particular developmental traits of the members of your audience.

An additional guideline for selecting literature to read aloud, then, is to base your selection of texts on the literary preferences of your audiences. The most direct way to make this determination is to ask your audience what their preferences are or otherwise survey them by employing some form of reading interest inventory. Unfortunately, the direct way does not always reveal the most valid results and may not be very practical. Children often respond by telling you what they think you want to hear rather than what they truly believe. Many public librarians may not know the precise constituency of their story hours from one week to the next. For them, even informal surveys are time-consuming and impractical.

Perhaps your best bet is to utilize available knowledge regarding the developmental needs, interests, and capabilities of people of different ages and then match these age traits with the themes you've identified in texts.

There are several good sources of information involving the developmental traits of children as it relates to the selection of literature consistent with those traits. One of the most extensive and convenient sources is in chart form and can be found in (Huck et al., 1997, pp. 52–59) *Children's Literature in the Elementary School.* Another can be found in (Norton, 1999, pp. 6–43) *Through the Eyes of a Child: An Introduction to Children's Literature.* For coverage of adolescent development and literature selection, you might review *Literature for Today's Young Adults* (Nilsen, 1995). Adults, as a group, are interested in and developmentally capable of dealing with the widest variety of literature, although their literary needs, interests, and capabilities may vary greatly from one person to another, even one situation to another. For example, they can enjoy listening to literature read aloud that is primarily appropriate for the very youngest child. However, they will do so, only in settings where the expectation is that they will be listening to children's literature.

Using your ability to identify literary or format elements, plus the information from the Huck and Nilsen texts, you can begin to match specific books with audiences of a specific age range. Consult Exampkes 2.3 and 2.4 for descriptions of the process in action.

Example 2.3

<u>Plot Concept, Theme–Trait Matching Process for *Rosie's Walk*</u>
(Page designations refer to Huck et al. *Children's Literature in the Elementary School*)

<u>Concept/Theme</u>	<u>Related Trait and Age Category</u>
Concept:	
hen, fox, farm landmarks	Age appropriateness can't be determined.
directional prepositions (over, under, around, etc.) Prepositional phrasing is a repeated pattern through out the text.	"Rapid development of language" (p. 52, Books for Ages & Stages: Preschool & Kindergarten– Ages 3, 4, & 5).
Theme:	
Good deeds are rewarded; bad deeds are punished.	"Makes absolute judgments about right and wrong" (p. 53, Books for Ages & Stages: Preschool & Kindergarten– Ages 3, 4, & 5).
Taking the initiative can be satisfying; being overly aggressive can lead to dissatisfaction.	"Beginning to assert independence" (p. 53, Books for Ages & Stages: Preschool & Kindergarten– Ages 3, 4, & 5).

Example 2.4

<u>Plot Concept, Theme–Trait Matching Process for *Pink and Say*</u>
(Page designations refer to Huck et al. *Children's Literature in the Elementary School*)

<u>Concept/Theme</u>	<u>Related Trait and Age Category</u>
Concept: past history	"Time concepts and spatial relationships developing." (p. 56, Books for Ages & Stages: Middle Elementary–Ages 8 & 9). "Increased understanding of the chronology of past events … " (p. 58, Books for Ages & Stages: Later Elementary–Ages 10 & 11).
intercultural relations	"Developing standards of right and wrong. Begins to see viewpoints of others" (p. 56, Books for Ages & Stages: Middle Elementary–Ages 8 & 9). "Searching for values; interested in problems of the world" (p. 58, Books for Ages & Stages: Later Elementary–Ages 10 & 11).
prejudicial behavior	Begins to see many dimensions of a problem." "Searching for values; interested in problems of the world. Can deal with abstract relationships; becoming more analytical" (p. 58, Books for Ages & Stages:

	Later Elementary – Ages 10 & 11).
Theme:	
Survival in an alien environment depends on the help one gets from others more familiar with the environment.	"Seeks to test own skills & abilities; looks ahead to a time of complete independence" (p. 57, Books for Ages & Stages: Later Elementary–Ages 10 & 11).
A person can be both afraid and brave at one and the same time.	Cognitive abilities are increasingly abstract and flexible ... " (p. 59, Books for Ages & Stages: Middle School–Ages 12, 13, & 14).
Being a just person does ensure that one will be treated justly by others.	"Sensitive to great complexity in human feelings and relationships" (p. 59, Books for Ages & Stages: Middle School–Ages 12, 13, & 14).

As mentioned before, theme–trait matching is probably the most accurate and convenient way of selecting literature to read aloud to specific audiences. Although plot topics, motifs, or even format elements such as the size of the print or the number of illustrations in a book may provide some clues as to the appropriateness of a text for a given audience, they can also be too superficial in attempting to make a definitive match-up. To say, for example, that *Charlotte's Web* is about farm animals or friendship isn't much help in determining an appropriate audience. Both *Who Sank the Boat* (Allen, 1982) and *Animal Farm* (Orwell, 1954) are about farm animals but would appeal to widely different audiences. Similarly, the friendship motif is found in books for audiences of all ages because friendship is a universal need of all people. To suggest that a major theme in *Charlotte's Web* is that true friendship involves responsibilities as well as privileges ties this story specifically to

6- to 8-year olds who, like Wilbur, are becoming less egocentric and more responsible individuals.

When preparing a read-aloud presentation that includes picture books, one special selection guideline should be followed. Because the illustrations are vitally important in communicating the fullest meaning of the book, they must be seen by all members of the audience. This rarely is a problem with small audiences (one to three people) because, typically, these people can gather close by the reader in full view of even the smallest illustrations. When audiences are larger, there will always be some distance between the reader and each audience member and that is when view-to-audience problems tend to crop up. In selecting books for larger audiences, you must consider the size and composition of the illustrations when judging view-to-audience.

Ask the following questions:

Are the illustrations large enough to be seen by all audience members?

Are the illustrations too detailed to be meaningful (or even to be minimally appreciated) by a large audience?

Does some aspect of the composition of the illustrations (color, tone, line, etc.) render the illustrations unintelligible at a distance?

It would be ridiculous to think of reading the nutshell library version of Sendak's (1962) *Pierre* to an audience of 30 children; the book measures only 2½" × 3¾". At first glance, however, it would be quite natural to think that Demi's (1998) *The Greatest Treasure* would be appropriate for this size of an audience. The book is large, and the illustrations are simple, bright, and colorful. But many of the illustrations are also very small. Much of the power of the story is lost when the audience can't see the facial expressions of the characters. You should be careful not to judge the appropriateness of a picture book purely on the dimensions of the book itself. Barton's (1995) *Tools* is small (5⅞" square), but the illustrations of the workers and their tools are very simple, surprisingly large for the size of the book, and easily distinguishable due to Barton's use of bright, contrasting colors for each of the elements in the pictures.

Books by illustrators such as Peter Spier and Steven Kellogg are frequently too detailed to be shared with large audiences. The illustrations in some books may be too light or too fine-lined to be seen at any distance: Williams' *Albert's Toothache* (1974) or Burningham's (1970) *Mr. Gumpy's Outing* (left-hand pages), for example. Still others might be too dark or harsh, as is the case with Mendez and Byard's (1989) *The Black Snowman.* In these in-stances, it would be better to share the books with individuals or small groups of children who are seated close at hand.

If you are in doubt about the visibility of the illustrations, prop the book open, have a friend hold it open, step back, and observe each illustration at a distance.

PREPARATION

It is natural, I suppose, for beginners at reading aloud to focus most attention on the performance because that is the moment of truth when you stand be-fore an audience and are expected to deliver the text to them with confi-dence, fluidity, and vitality. However, the quality of your performance will depend primarily on the quality of your preparation prior to the perfor-mance. In fact, thorough preparation is what transforms the nondescript acts of reading lines from a text into an art form—a thing of beauty. As such, the major focus of your attention should be on the preparation.

Whether you are a beginning or experienced reader, you cannot afford to wait until the performance to make the majority of delivery decisions. Even with the simplest picture book, there will be too many decisions to make with regard to its presentation to wait until the time of performance. Ques-tions involving exposure of the illustrations; handling of books of varying sizes, shapes, or formats; book movement; handling unique arrangements of texts on pages; pronunciation of unusual words; articulation of awkward syntactic structures; and questions about your own personal appearance must be resolved as you prepare for a performance. Postponing deliberation of these questions until the moment of performance typically results in un-necessary anxiety and a loss of confidence on the part of the reader and a flawed performance. Conversely, dealing with these questions via thorough preparation prior to performance tends to bolster your confidence and en-sure a successful presentation.

Three things must be analyzed in preparing for a picture book perfor-mance: the illustrations, the text, and oneself.

Analysis of Illustrations

You can utilize the following list of questions as a guide in analyzing the illus-trations of a picture book you are considering for reading aloud to an audi-ence.

Will any important elements of the illustrations be difficult to see?
Does the format of the illustrations present any unique viewing
   problems?
Does the format of the book present any unique viewing problems?
Do the illustrations call for any special effects?

Certainly, if you believe that too many important elements of the illustrations won't be seen by members of your potential audience, the book should not be selected for that performance. Suppose that only one or two elements are of concern and can't be seen for some unusual reason, what then? I've found, for example, that children often don't see the face of the baby mouse peeking onto the right-hand edge of the second to last picture in Kraus' (1970) *Whose Mouse Are You?* perhaps because the picture of the older brother mouse so dominates the illustration. The first solution to this problem is to expose this illustration for a longer than normal time, thus enabling some children to follow the natural line of the older mouse's tail that points directly to the baby. If that fails, I will often run the index finger of my free hand under the older brother's tail from left to right stopping just underneath the baby's face.

Invariably the children will follow along with their eyes. Finger pointing, used judiciously, can be a very effective technique. It can be used on page 23 of Lionni's (1969) *Alexander and the Wind-Up Mouse* to point out the magic purple pebble that is located in a less-than-obvious spot close to the gutter of the book and the bottom of the page and nearly surrounded by the dark shadowing of a box. It can be used with Balian's (1997) *Humbug Rabbit* to distinguish among the many characters and important setting elements exposed in the first four pages of text. It can be employed with Andrews' (1985) *Very Last First Time* to expose children to the figures of various animals that Ian Wallace has cleverly hidden in the ice formations on several pages. Be careful not to overuse finger pointing, however. As a general rule, the least amount of finger pointing, the better. If you find you have to point to an abundance of elements in the illustrations, it's likely that the book is not an appropriate selection for this audience at this time.

In some books, the format of the illustrations can be a concern or, at least, an interesting challenge to the reader. Because the cost of producing a picture book can be quite expensive, publishers frequently lower their production costs by publishing a book where the pages alternate from colored to black and white illustrations. Briggs' (1970) *Jim and the Beanstalk* is a good example. The problem is that not all the black and white illustrations are as interesting or as discernible at a distance as are the colored illustrations.

However, the story is delightful, and the size and composition of the colored illustrations make the book a good read-aloud text. How then should the black and white illustrations be handled? By contrast, Aruego's picture of the mother mouse caught inside the cat in *Whose Mouse Are You?* (Kraus, 1970) is no problem at all: The picture is big and bright, and audiences are usually quick to identify the mouse's tail protruding from the cat's mouth. How can the reading of this page augment the natural drama Aruego injects into the illustration?

In the case of both of these books, a solution is to employ book movement. With the Brigg's text, as I move from a page with a colored illustration to a page with a black and white illustration, I turn the book inward to my body so that the audience cannot see the black and white illustration. I read all the text on that page, then turn the page and continue reading to an appropriate spot. I then stop reading at that point and expose the colored illustration to the audience. With the Kraus-Aruego book, I turn it inward toward my body when I've finished reading the text on the page prior to the one with the cat illustration. I then turn the page to the one with the cat on it and quickly turn the book outward to face the audience as I read the words, "Inside the cat," thus exposing, in a surprise fashion, the cat illustration. This approach has always been received with much delight by child and adult audiences alike.

Beyond the format of the illustrations, the overall format of the book may also present the reader with certain problems. Hardcover versions of texts are often larger than their paperback counterparts [my hardcover copy of *Crow Boy* (Yashima, 1955) measures 9¼" x 12⅜"; the Scholastic paperback measures 7½" x 9"] and are typically more substantial as well. This situation is both a blessing and a burden. The pages of a hardcover text won't fall out as easily as they will in a paperback. Large audiences will be better able to see the larger illustrations in the hardcover. But the hardcover texts will also be heavier than paperbacks, and many of them will be side-sewn so that some important aspects of the illustrations may be buried in the gutter of the book. Keeping side-sewn hardbacks wide open and preventing pages from flopping inward, thus interfering with an audience's full view of the illustrations, is a problem—a problem shared with most paperbacks, which are bound at the spine so tightly with glue that the pages can't be opened up flat. I refer to these books as *stiffs*.

Prevention of these picture book format problems involves choosing a hand-holding position that provides both maximum exposure of the illustrations to the audience and maximum security so that the book doesn't fall from your hand or waver uncontrollably. Consider the logic of the following positions demonstrated in Example 2.5.

Example 2.5

Hand-Holding Positions

Position 1

Hold the book to the
side of your body with
one hand positioned at
the top of the book.

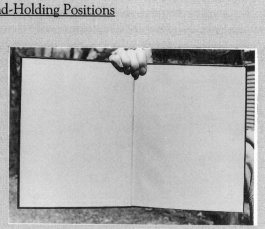

Logic

Gravity pulls the book down and away from your hand. Securing the
book requires considerable hand squeezing, which can become tiresome
and painful.

Position 2

Hold the book in front
of your body with two
hands positioned at the
top, on the sides, or
underneath the book.

Logic

Reading the text is difficult; you must crane your neck over the top
of the book and be able to read upside down.

Position 3

> Hold the book to the side of
> your body with two hands in a
> variety of positions.

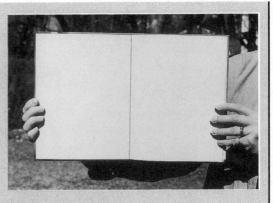

Logic

Awkward positioning that interferes either with your view of the
text or the audience's view of the illustrations.

Position 4

> Hold the book to the side of
> your body with one hand
> positioned to the left or right
> of the book gutter.

Logic

The book, especially if it is a *stiff*, tends to flop closed, thus preventing
full view to the audience.

Position 5

> Hold the book to the side of
> your body with one hand
> positioned at the center and
> bottom of the book; the
> thumb and little finger
> are in front and the three
> middle fingers are behind
> the book.

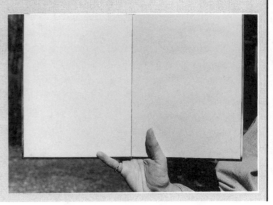

Logic

Insecure position especially with tall or wide books; limited ability to open the book flat. With *stiffs*, the book tends to flop shut.

Position 6

Hold the book to the side of your body with one hand positioned at the center and bottom of the book; the four fingers are in front and spread evenly across the book gutter; the heel of the hand and the thumb are behind the book .

Logic

Secure position. Working with gravity not against it; enables you to press the book open as flat as possible and hold the book up high or low while sitting or standing.

In the final analysis, this sixth position appears to be the best all-around position for both view-to-audience and security purposes. Even with this position, however, it may be that, with a *stiff*, the pages tend to buckle up on you as you turn farther and farther into the book. To prevent this buckling up, as you turn to each new page and simultaneously release your four fingers to permit this turning, try pressing the two pages flat using the whole of your free hand and then tightly regrasp the book with your four fingers. Be certain that your fingers aren't covering any important elements of the illustrations.

The major concern with a large, heavy picture book is that your arm will tire from holding it up in a single position for any length of time. To deal with these *heavies*, you may want to employ a side-to-side sweeping movement, perhaps even switching the book from one hand to the other. This movement will prevent cramping in your arm and eliminate any distracting and unintentional book wavering. The trick here is to identify appropriate spots in the text where stopping the reading to expose the illustrations in this manner poses no problem to text flow. Having identified those spots, be sure to complete the sweep slowly and steadily to provide the audience with sufficient exposure to the illustrations. Also avoid covering your face with the book. Sweep the book below your face so that you maintain continued eye contact with the audience.

Analysis of Text

Having analyzed the illustrations, you can now turn your attention to the words on the pages. Begin this analysis by reading over the text silently then out loud several times. This out-loud reading is critical because it is only when you read the text in this way that you discover textual peculiarities that prevent your delivering the text fluently to an audience.

Use the following questions to analyze the text:

Are some elements of the text located in nontypical parts of the page (buried in the illustrations, for example) or arranged on the page in some unique manner?
Should the text be altered in any way?
Is the print large enough to be easily seen?
Do units of text flow from one page to the next?
Are some elements of the text difficult for you to speak?
Do any textual elements require special effects (mood, sounds, music, atypical pronunciations, etc.)?

Typically the words to be read in a picture book are clumped together in one spot on each page and are easily located. But with some books, finding the next line to read can be difficult. In *Crow Boy* (Yashima, 1955), cited earlier, most of the text appears at the bottom of the page. Having read the first four pages with no variation in this pattern and then turning to the fifth page, it is easy to miss the line of print about half way up the page that reads, "He was left alone in the study time." Note why it is easy to skip this line. First, the text on the fourth page ("He was afraid of the children and could not make friends with them at all") could lead naturally to the text at the bottom of the fifth page ("He was left alone in the play time") as well as to the text half way up the page. Second, Yashima changed the format of the illustrations for the first time on the fifth page, moving from a single picture per page to two pictures per page, one stacked on top of the other. Handling this transition and the potential problem of skipping important text simply involves concentration at the time of performance. However, concentration can be improved prior to the performance by careful preparation. In this case, practice slowing down the pace of your reading. This allows you enough time to first survey each new page and locate the next line of print to be read before having to actually read the text.   .

Unlike *Crow Boy*, it is not difficult to find all the text to be read in *Dandelion* (Freeman, 1964). The question here is whether you should read aloud all the text provided. Should you read the letter on Page 8, the signs on

Pages 11, 17, 19, and 22, and the magazine text on page 15? The question can be resolved by studying these unique textual elements, determining whether they augment or hinder text flow, and then editing out those that interfere with the flow. In *Dandelion*, it is essential to read the letter on Page 8. Otherwise the audience won't know what causes Dandelion's excitement referred to on Page 9. But the sign and magazine texts are not essential textual elements and cannot be worked into the basic text without interrupting its natural flow. These elements should not be read aloud during the performance of the text.

Extensive text editing should be avoided if at all possible; simply choose not to read texts that require major alterations. Now and then, however, there may be an exception. Such is the case for me with de Paola's (1978) *Bill and Pete*. I enjoy the story up to the page where William Everett Crocodile shows his mother that he can write his own name. The text that follows this page seems anticlimactic and irrelevant to the basic plot line. As such, I simply end the story by turning the book inward toward me on Page 17, turning to Page 18, and reading the first two sentences, " 'Did you learn something today, William Everett?' asked Mama. 'Yes, Mama, I learned to write my name,' said William Everett." With the book still turned inward, I then ask the audience: "And how do you suppose William Everett spelled his name?" The audience response of "Bill" completes the story.

Another text that involves major reorganization and some slight deletion for reading aloud is Balian's (1997) *Humbug Rabbit*. Because of the unique parallel format of the book where two stories are taking place simultaneously on each page (one above ground, the other below), only Pages 5 (the first page with text), 6, 8, 9, 21, and 28 through 32 can be read in the standard way—left page first, then right, and top to bottom. To maintain the meaningful sequence of the story, most of the double-page spreads must be read so that all of the text on either the top or bottom half of the page is read together. At times, the bottom half text must be read before the top half. Also in this story, I make two small textual changes (switching the order of "Father and Mother Rabbit" on Page 5 and the order of the two sentences on Page 7) and one deletion (the text on the last page, which, in my experience, is received by audiences as anticlimactic). Compare the actual text sequence (following a strict left-to-right, top-to-bottom progression) with the read-aloud text sequence in the story that follows.

Humbug Rabbit

(Illustration)

This is Granny
And the house she lives in.

(Illustration)

This is Father and Mother Rabbit
and the burrow they live in.

Read: This is Granny and the house she lives in. This is Mother and Father Rabbit and the burrow they live in.

This is Otto, the rooster
who tells the sun and Granny
when it is time to get up in the morning.

(Illustration)

(Illustration)

This is Granny's chicken coop
and her hen, Gracie, who lays one egg every day

This is Barnaby, a most devilish cat.

(Illustration)

(Illustration)

These are the five Rabbit children.

This is a mouse.

Read: This is Otto the rooster who tells the sun and Granny when it is time to get up in the morning. This is Granny's chicken coop and her hen, Gracie, who lays one egg every day. These are the five Rabbit children. This is a mouse. This is Barnaby, a most devilish cat.

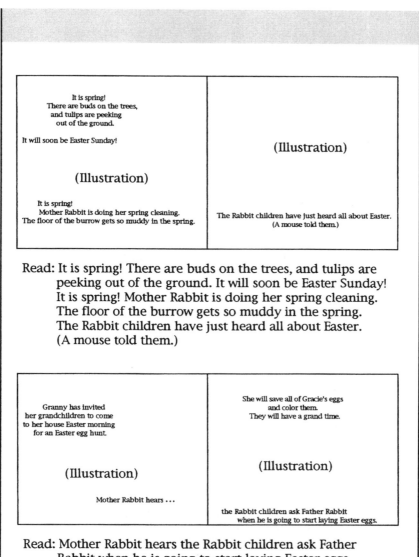

It is spring!
There are buds on the trees,
and tulips are peeking
out of the ground.

It will soon be Easter Sunday!

(Illustration)

It is spring!
Mother Rabbit is doing her spring cleaning.
The floor of the burrow gets so muddy in the spring.

(Illustration)

The Rabbit children have just heard all about Easter.
(A mouse told them.)

Read: It is spring! There are buds on the trees, and tulips are peeking out of the ground. It will soon be Easter Sunday! It is spring! Mother Rabbit is doing her spring cleaning. The floor of the burrow gets so muddy in the spring. The Rabbit children have just heard all about Easter. (A mouse told them.)

Granny has invited
her grandchildren to come
to her house Easter morning
for an Easter egg hunt.

(Illustration)

Mother Rabbit hears ...

She will save all of Gracie's eggs
and color them.
They will have a grand time.

(Illustration)

the Rabbit children ask Father Rabbit
when he is going to start laying Easter eggs.

Read: Mother Rabbit hears the Rabbit children ask Father Rabbit when he is going to start laying Easter eggs. Granny has invited her grandchildren to come to her house Easter morning for an Easter egg hunt. She will save all of Gracie's eggs and color them. They will have a grand time.

| But Alas!

(Illustration)

The Rabbit children believe
their Father is the Easter Bunny.
(The mouse told them so.) | Gracie has stopped laying eggs!
Granny has searched the chicken coop,
and there is no egg today.

(Illustration)

Father Rabbit tells them that that is absurd!
"There is no Easter Bunny!" he says.
"And rabbits do not lay eggs!" he says. |

Read: But Alas! Gracie has stopped laying eggs. Granny has searched the chicken coop, and there is no egg today. The Rabbit children believe their father is the Easter Bunny. (The mouse told them so.) Father Rabbit tells them that that is absurd! "There is no Easter Bunny!" he says. "And rabbits do not lay eggs!" he says.

| There have been no eggs
for days and days.

Granny is worried.

(Illustration)

The Rabbit children are very excited!
They KNOW their father is the Easter Bunny.
(Remember what the mouse said?) | She is worried that Gracie might be ill.

She is worried that there will be no eggs
for the Easter egg hunt.

(Illustration)

Father Rabbit tells them it is all humbug.
"That mouse is a fool!" he says.
"RABBITS DO NOT LAY EGGS!" he says. |

Read: The Rabbit children are very excited! They KNOW their father is the Easter Bunny. (Remember what the mouse said?) Father Rabbit tells them it is all humbug. "That mouse is a fool!" he says. "RABBITS DO NOT LAY EGGS!" he says. There have been no eggs for days and days. Granny is worried. She is worried that Gracie might be ill. She is worried that there will be no eggs for the Easter egg hunt.

Surprise!
Granny discovers a whole nest
full of eggs.

(Illustration)

The Rabbit children help their mother make carrot
cookies. They tell her that they will leave a plate of
cookies and a nice cup of lettuce juice on the table on
Easter Eve-

(That devilish cat, Barnaby, showed her
where Gracie had been hiding them
under the chicken coop.)

She is so happy
but scolds Gracie
for worrying her like that.

(Illustration)

for their father, who is the Easter Bunny.

Read: Surprise! Granny discovers a whole nest full of eggs. (That devilish cat, Barnaby, showed her where Gracie had been hiding them under the chicken coop.) She is so happy but scolds Gracie for worrying her like that. The Rabbit children help their mother make carrot cookies. They tell her that they will leave a plate of cookies and a nice cup of lettuce juice on the table on Easter Eve- for their father, who is the Easter Bunny.

Granny busily paints
and decorates eggs.

(Illustration)

Father Rabbit tells his family that he does not want to
hear any more Easter Bunny nonsense!

(Illustration)

"HUMBUG!" he says.
"FOOLISHNESS!" he says.

Read: Father Rabbit tells his family that he does not want to hear any more Easter Bunny nonsense! "HUMBUG!" he says. "FOOLISHNESS!" he says. Granny busily paints and decorates eggs.

(Illustration)

It is the night before Easter, and Granny has
hidden all the colored Easter eggs in the tall grass.
Barnaby, that devilish cat, waits until Granny
goes to bed and then pushes all the beautifully
painted eggs down the rabbit holes.

(Illustration)

Read: It is the night before Easter, and Granny has   hidden all the
      colored Easter eggs in the tall grass. Barnaby, that devilish cat,
      waits until Granny goes to bed and then pushes all the
      beautifully painted eggs down the rabbit holes.

It is Easter morning,
and Granny's grandchildren arrive.
They are happy to see her
and eager to hunt
for Easter eggs.

(Illustration)

(Illustration)

It is Easter morning, and there is
much excitement in the rabbit burrow.

The Rabbit children have discovered
the Easter eggs!

Read: It is Easter morning, and Granny's grandchildren arrive. They
      are happy to see her and eager to hunt for Easter eggs. It is
      Easter morning, and there is much excitement in the rabbit
      burrow. The Rabbit children have discovered the Easter eggs!

Granny is puzzled.
What kind of an Easter egg hunt
is this?

(Illustration)

Her grandchildren have looked everywhere
and have not found even one of the eggs!

(Illustration)

Father Rabbit is puzzled.
THERE ARE EASTER EGGS HATCHING
ALL OVER HIS BURROW!

Read: Granny is puzzled. What kind of an Easter egg hunt is this? Her grandchildren have looked everywhere and have not found even one of the eggs! Father Rabbit is puzzled. THERE ARE EASTER EGGS HATCHING ALL OVER HIS BURROW!

Suddenly, Granny's yard is all afluter
with peeping chicks, hopping rabbits,
and giggling grandchildren.

(Illustration)

(Illustration)

Mother Rabbit shoos her children outside
to play with the new baby chicks

and tries to soothe Father Rabbit
with a quiet breakfast of carrot cookies and lettuce
juice.

Read: Mother Rabbit shoos her children outside to play with the new baby chicks and tries to soothe Father Rabbit with a quiet breakfast of carrot cookies and lettuce juice. Suddenly Granny's yard is all aflutter with peeping chicks, hopping rabbits, and giggling grandchildren.

It is a happy Easter for Granny and her grandchildren (Illustration)	and for Gracie and Otto. (Illustration) The Rabbit children are so proud of their father. They knew he was the Easter Bunny. (The mouse told them so.)

Read: It is a happy Easter for Granny and her grandchildren and for Gracie and Otto. The Rabbit children are so proud of their father. They knew he was the Easter Bunny. (The mouse told them so.)

It is the end of a lovely Easter Day. (Illustration) Mother Rabbit and her children have covered their muddy floor with the colored egg shells, and it looks just lovely.	(Illustration) Father Rabbit is wondering if he really is the EASTER BUNNY.

Read: It is the end of a lovely Easter Day. Mother Rabbit and her children have covered their muddy floor with the colored egg shells, and it looks just lovely. Father Rabbit is wondering if he really is the EASTER BUNNY.

Read: "I told you so!" says the mouse.

If the print on a page is relatively small or if there is an abundance of print on a single page, as is the case on many of the pages in *Amos and Boris* (Steig, 1971) or *Jim and the Beanstalk* (Briggs, 1970), to avoid losing your place, you may want to read the text with the illustrations facing you, then at appropriate points stop the reading and expose the illustrations to your audience. Again, careful preparation is the key to success. Knowing when to expose each picture and how much exposure time to provide each picture without destroying the timing or flow of the text are decisions that must be made prior to the performance. Having made these decisions, you may want to use light pencil marks in the book itself to remind you when to expose an illustration.

You must pay special attention to text that flows from one page to the next, particularly if page turning is required. Practice moving your eyes to the new text and turning the page early so that you don't interrupt the text flow with an unnatural pause.

You may find as you practice reading out loud that certain words or phrases are difficult for you to articulate. Perhaps it's the word *aminal* in Balian's (1972) story of the same name, the phrase "A walrus mustache" in *My Daddy's Mustache* (Salus, 1979) or the sentence "I put my mittens over the scarf over my mouth and listened hard" in Yolen's (1987a) *Owl Moon*. Maybe it's the text of an entire book, one written in a dialect somewhat foreign to you, such as McKissack's (1986) *Flossie and the Fox*. If you truly enjoy these books and want to share them with audiences, you'll have to work to eliminate the articulation problems—a relatively simple mater for small problems, a major undertaking for large ones. For small problems, you may find that slight overenunciation works for you, but a better bet is to simply slow the pace way down when you are about to read these difficult parts. Clearly, mastering an entire text that presents you with articulation problems will require extensive practice, working with small units of text at a time.

As you become more accomplished at reading aloud to audiences, you will want to begin matching the pacing of your reading to the natural pace of the text. Most books begin at a moderate pace then speed up or slow down as the situation warrants. In *Mr. Gumpy's Outing* (Burningham, 1970), for example, the pace is steady and moderate as all the characters climb aboard the boat. But then on a single page, the pace changes from moderate to rapid, ending with an elliptical pause:

> For a little while they all went along happily
> but then ...
> The goat kicked

>The calf trampled
>The chickens flapped
>The sheep bleated
>The pig mucked about
>The dog teased the cat
>The cat chased the rabbit
>The rabbit hopped
>The children squabbled
>The boat tipped ...

You want to speed up your reading rate to match this pace change but not become so rapid that articulation suffers. Practicing this rate change will lead to perfection.

Pausing can also be used as a tool to alter pace; it is one of the most dramatic tools available to the reader. Pausing at the second ellipsis in the text cited earlier, for example, enables you to slow the pace back to moderate to conclude the sentence with the words "and into the water they fell." The effect of this pause and pace change is very dramatic and in perfect synchronization with the high drama of the text. Use pausing, as well, to create a mood of anticipation or heightened suspense as would be the case if you were to pause at the first ellipsis in the previous text. Prior to performance, you want to plan carefully where to pause for dramatic effect in the texts you will be reading. Do avoid overuse of this technique, however, for overuse reduces its dramatic effect.

Pacing and pausing are two of the more prominent special effects called for when reading a text, but there are many others. Some books require the reader to make special sounds: the sounds of birds in *Crow Boy* (Yashima, 1955) and *Owl Moon* (Yolen, 1987a), of an old-time auto horn in *Piggins* (Yolen, 1987b) or of train whistles in *Train Whistles* (Sattler, 1985), for example. You must first ask yourself if you can replicate these sounds in a natural and authentic manner and not appear silly or phony doing so. If you feel you can't make the sounds and there is no compelling reason for you to have to use them, simply edit the sounds out of your reading. If deleting these sounds would somehow significantly alter the meaning of the text, then your choices are either to eliminate the book from your repertoire or practice making the sounds to the point where you feel confident using them in your reading. This guideline also applies to books such as *Lizard's Song* (Shannon, 1981), which incorporate songs into their texts.

Mood changes or variations in emotion, changes in speakers when dialogue is incorporated into the text, or radical changes in syntax all can be effectively dealt with by varying voice volume, pitch, tone, or rhythm. The text of *White Dynamite and Curly Kidd* (Martin & Archambault, 1986) opens with Lucky Kidd talking to Curly, her father, just before he is to ride a mean bull at the rodeo. Lucky is excited and frightened for her father all at the same time. Curly is calm and cool. Obviously, the vocal representation of these two characters must be different. Lucky's voice might be pitched high, loud, and somewhat shaky befitting her nervousness. Curly's voice could be pitched lower, quieter, and steadier as is appropriate for his state of mind. But this opening dialogue extends for many pages and rapidly switches back and forth between Lucky and Curly.

> Here comes Dynamite, Dad.
> > Yep.
> They're puttin' him in the chute.
> > Yep.
> He sure looks mean.
> > He's mean all right.
> But a mean bull means extra points.
> > Yep.
> So you were lucky to get him, huh?
> > Yep, luck of the draw.
> They say he's the meanest bull
> in the whole United States.
> > Yep.
> But you're the best bull rider
> in the whole United States
> … and Canada, huh?
> > Could be.

Thus, the reader will have to thoroughly practice the rapid vocal variation required to successfully handle this dialogue. Later in the story, when Curly is riding the bull and Lucky is watching while thinking out loud, the rhyming and rhythmic patterns used to represent her thoughts change rapidly.

> Oh!
> He's outa the chute!
> Gone plumb dumb wild!
> > KAN-sas
> > TEX-as
> > U-tah
> > MAINE

That bull's pitchin'
with all his might ...
twenty-four tons
a' White Dynamite!

Stick with 'im, Dad!
    AL-a-BAM-a
    MINN-e-SOT-a
    IN-di-AN-a
    AR-i-ZO-na

Leapin' like a bull frog ...
    O-ma_HA ne-BRAS-ka
Dustin' up the Big Sky ...
    KET-chi-KAN a-LAS-ka
Landin' hard
    new MEX-i-CO

Four seconds down, DAD!
Four more to go!

These changes are tricky and require a great deal of concentration during
the performance aided by an abundance of practice beforehand.

Analysis of Self

You can't afford to stop the analysis once you've surveyed the illustrations
and the text. You must also analyze your own person as you would appear
before your audience.

   Think about the following questions:

   Will the audience members likely be distracted as they
        listen to me read?
   Will I interfere with the audience's view
        of the illustrations?
   How will I establish and maintain audience
        control?
   How will I know how the audience is
        responding to my story?

When you are reading a picture book to an audience, the center of attention should be the book and not you. Neither your clothing nor personal appearance and mannerisms should distract the audience from the book. Be particularly cautious of dangling or gaudy jewelry and hair styles that partially cover your eyes or obscure your view of the audience. Some natural gesturing and facial expression is likely to take place when you are reading a particularly emotional segment, but you should limit your gesturing and control facial expression. This is no time for mugging at the audience or acting out the story with body movement. Eliminate distracting physical and vocal tics from your presence. Be careful of excessive leg swinging if you are seated with one leg crossed over the other and avoid unplanned lip smacking or tongue clicking as you read. Let your voice alone carry the motion of the text.

Plan to anchor yourself firmly in one spot where all the members of the audience can see the illustrations. Your posture doesn't have to be stiff or formal; you should be relaxed physically, but not slouching to the point where you can't breathe comfortably or are the attraction the audience is observing and not the book. If you are standing, keep your feet spread apart at about hip width and avoid swaying from side to side or back and forth.

It makes no difference whether you stand or sit to read as long as the audience has a clear and unobstructed view of the illustrations. As such, the book should be above the level of audience members' heads. Position yourself so that your body doesn't block their view. Be looking and listening for feedback from the audience that suggests that they can't see the illustrations (e.g., necks craning, unaccountable restlessness, lack of attention to the illustrations, talking).

Suppose you are reading a book with lots of text but illustrations that require continual and extensive exposure. It is likely that you will turn the book inward toward your body to get a better view of the text—a natural instinct. But if you do so and are positioned at the midpoint in front of your audience and up close to them, it may be that some members on the book side of your audience may not be able to see the illustrations. Correct the situation by moving slightly back from the audience and all the way over to the last row of audience members to the book side. In this position, you can turn the book inward to get a better view of the text, and all the audience members will be able to see the illustrations.

Be careful not to let parts of your body (especially hands and arms) interfere with the audience's view of the illustrations. In some books, it's very easy for your holding hand to block an important part of an illustration even when your hand is in the proper position [e.g., covering the purple pebble on Page 23 of *Alexander and the Wind-Up Mouse* (Lionni, 1969)]. In this situation (or if you have very long fingers), you may have to practice curling your fingers a bit to avoid them protruding too far onto the page. In general, you want to keep your free hand down at your side or in your lap until you need to use it to turn the page. In this way, you won't inadvertently cover some important element of the illustrations.

There are two basic reasons that you want to make eye contact with your audience. Control of an audience is established and maintained primarily through eye contact. But also remember that reading aloud is a form of communication, which is a two-way process. You can learn a great deal about how your audience members are receiving what is being read if you look at them and learn to read their faces and body language. This feedback, in turn, can help you alter you interpretation of the text.

Remember that you are receiving as well as sending information. The general guidelines for eye contact are simple: the more, the better as long as you can maintain the flow of the reading. Be sure to establish some eye contact with all parts of your audience over the course of reading an entire book, and let your head movement be slow and smooth rather than quick and jerky. Obviously, getting your eyes off the text and out into the audience for any length of time is going to require careful planing and practice. You must determine where you can break eye contact with the text and how you will reestablish that contact when you need to resume the reading. But this task is easily accomplished because your mind can monitor the print five to seven words in advance of the text being produced orally.

So begin by working with the ends of text units such as paragraphs or pages. Decide where in the last sentence of a paragraph you can actually lift your eyes from the text, and look at the audience while continuing to read aloud to the end of the sentence. Use the same technique when reading the last few words on the right-hand page so you can turn the page while looking at the audience yet maintaining the flow of the oral reading. Conscious attention must also be paid to reestablishing focus on the text so as to avoid losing your place. Once you have identified the spots where you can leave and reenter the text, you may find it useful to mark them with a light pencil line.

Do consider techniques for introducing the story and, if necessary, for following up the reading with some extension activity. You should always announce the author and illustrator, but you may not necessarily want to do this before reading the text. It may be to your advantage to provide this information after the reading. For example, introducing the title of Williams' (1973) *Petronella* beforehand might undermine the suspense and inherent predictability of the plot (that the *knight* who is determined to seek his fortune turns out to be female). Better to save this title until after the reading.

Review appropriate sections of children's and adolescent literature text books for descriptions of potential follow-up activities.

Putting It All Together

Once you've completed your analyses of the illustrations, text, and self, and you have made various decisions as to how you will actually present the book to an audience, you must then implement these decisions and practice reading the book exactly as you planned it, in its entirety, and out loud. Don't be fooled into believing that you can practice reading the text only in parts or silently and still attain oral fluidity. It simply won't happen. At some point when you are reading the text fluidly, time several practice readings with a stopwatch and record the average time it takes to complete the text from start to finish. This information will come in handy later when organizing for a specific performance. You may want to record other information about your story as well. You can use the sample form provided or devise one of your own (see Fig. 2.1).

Figure 2.1

Read Aloud Picture Book

Book Title:_____

Author/Illustrator:_____

Publisher/Date of Publication:_____

Location of Book:_____

Average Time to Read Book:_____

Intended Audience:_____

Rationale (Employ Plot Concept, Theme-Trait Matching Process):

Personal Appeal (State why the book interests you personally beyond any utilitarian value):

Story Preparation (List potential problems and solutions in each area):

Illustration Analysis:

Text Analysis:

Self-Analysis:

A few words about the use of audio- or video-recording devices or mirrors during practice. Although I believe these aids can be of great value in self-analyzing your performance, I typically don't recommend their use for beginners. Far too frequently, the beginner focuses on all the wrong things—the general tonal quality of one's voice with audiotapes and one's general appearance with videotapes and mirrors. Usually the self-judgment is negative and discouraging and serves only to distract you from the important business at hand. The time to use recorders and mirrors (if at all necessary) is after you've developed a level of self-confidence as a reader that enables you to look beyond the superficial to the more important elements of selection, preparation, and delivery discussed in this chapter.

DELIVERY

If your preparation has been thorough, your delivery will be successful because you will have attained a sufficient level of confidence through practice to present the picture book to the audience. However, there are some things you can do immediately prior to and during your performance to galvanize its success.

What to Do Prior to Delivery

If you are not satisfied with the arrangement of the audience, change it if you are able to prior to the reading. If you are reading to a class of children, for example, and they are scattered around the room at their desks, request that they all move to an open area of the room and sit on the floor close by you. Direct individual children into place so that they all can see the illustrations. If you cannot rearrange your audience and conditions are less than perfect, quickly think how you might compensate for the problems. For example, if the audience is very close to you but some members are seated far to your left or right, you may have to walk back and forth as you expose each illustration—no problem as long as your movement is slow and steady.

As a beginner, you may be a bit nervous the first several times you perform. If so, pause before you begin reading and take a deep, relaxing, but imperceptible breath and concentrate on delivering the story just as you practiced it.

What to Do During the Delivery

Handling overt audience reaction (particularly with child audiences) is situational in nature. If you have prepared a book that calls for audience participation, such as Roffey's (1982) *Home Sweet Home* ("Do butterflies live in a hive? No! Bees live in a hive"), or one with such a highly predictable text that it invites participation, such as Ginsburg's (1972) *The Chick and the Duckling* ("I found a worm," said the Duckling. "Me too," said the Chick. "I caught a butterfly," said the Duckling. "Me too," said the Chick.), you won't be surprised when the audience begins to "recite" the text out loud along with you. You will have thought of ways to signal the audience to stop reading if there is a need to do so [leaning toward the audience and simultaneously raising the intonation to a high level on the word where they should stop reading, as on the word "five" in this excerpt from *Inch by Inch* (Lionni, 1960)—"That's easy," said the inch worm. "One, two, three, four, *five* inches.")]. For interruptions, sometimes the best thing to do is ignore them.

As mentioned before, pausing is an attention-getter. Typically when you pause, the members of the audience, including the persons causing the distractions, will direct their attention to your face. Then you can use direct eye contact with the distracters to control their behavior. If at all possible, avoid stopping the reading to admonish the distracter. A better technique would be to inject the person's name into the text at an appropriate spot and continue the reading while making frequent eye contact with the distracter. Stop the reading to admonish someone only as a last resort because to do so will surely destroy the flow and enjoyment of the story for the audience members who are attending to your reading.

BIG BOOKS

The use of commercially produced *big books* has gained in popularity in the past decade. Young children develop valuable concepts about print (for more information on *concepts about print*, see Clay, 1979) when they are able to view the text being read aloud along with the illustrations in a book. But seeing the text in a standard sized book, even a large one, is questionable in a classroom setting where, for convenience, large groups of children must be read to at any one time. Big books solve this problem, but create other logistical problems for the person reading them aloud.

Too large and floppy to be hand-held, big books must be placed on some support surface. For small groups of five or six children, the big book can be spread out on the floor with the audience and reader gathering in front of it. But for large groups, the book will have to be propped up on an easel or stand high enough so that all audience members can see the entirety of each page. If the easel has no broad backing to support the full width of a big book, purchase an inexpensive piece of fibreboard (2' by 3' is sufficient) from your local lumber yard and prop that up on the easel to serve as back support for the book.

Because the binding of a new big book will be stiff, loosen it up before reading the text by opening the book to each page and rubbing your hand firmly up and down the book gutter until the pages lie flat.

Because it is important for young children to make the connection between the print text in the book and the oral text being verbalized, consider using a pointer when reading rather than your finger. In this way, you can stand beside the book and read and point to the text without blocking the audience's view of the print text with your body.

EXTENDED PRACTICE ACTIVITIES

Developmental Activities

Using a collection of books (at a public or school library or one provided by the instructor of your course or workshop) where appropriate, choose from this list those activities that you find helpful in improving your ability to select, prepare, and deliver picture books to an audience via reading aloud. If possible, complete the exercises with a friend.

1. Distinguish picture books from nonpicture books.

2. Using the guidelines on Page 8, analyze the format of several different books and determine in general what age person they would be appropriate for.

3. Identify the topical content for a sample book or two. By looking at the list of topics covered in a single book, is it possible for you to identify what age person might find this book interesting?

4. Using the directives on Page 9 and few sample books, identify some themes in each of the books.

5. Using the chart provided in the *Children's Literature in the Elementary School* (Huck et al., 1997, pp. 52–59) and some picture books, employ the Plot Concept, Theme–Trait Matching Process to identify what age child the books would be appropriate for. You may want to begin by discussing concepts and themes for *Rosie's Walk* and *Pink and Say* not discussed in this chapter.

6. Survey some picture books to determine whether the illustrations can be clearly seen at a distance of 20 feet.

7. Take a single picture book and, utilizing the questions on Page 15, analyze the illustrations.

8. Using a picture book, practice holding the book and turning the pages (don't bother reading the text for the time being) so that you provide full, steady exposure of the illustrations to an imaginary audience. Better still,

complete this exercise with a small group of friends where the friends act as the audience. Practice preventing the pages from buckling up as you turn from one page to he next. Also practice switching the book from one hand to another and moving the book slowly in front of an imaginary audience.

9. Choose a large picture book and try the various hand-holding positions described in Example 2.5. Determine which position is the least strenuous and most secure.

10. Take a single picture book and, utilizing the questions on Page 22, analyze the text.

11. Repeat Exercise 8, but this time read the text out loud. Note those spots where you are having trouble with fluency and determine how you might solve these problems.

12. Using a single picture book, locate spots in the text where it would be natural to pause in reading for dramatic effect; to change the pace of your reading; to vary the volume, pitch, tone, or rhythm of your reading.

13. Find a picture book with a simple, short text. Practice reading the text out loud while making slow, smooth, and extensive eye contact with all members of an imaginary audience (or real audience of peers). If a real audience is used, direct them to do things such as making faces, scratching their noses, closing their eyes, staring off into space, and so on while you are reading. See how many of their unusual gestures you notice. The intent here is to improve your ability to monitor audience reaction to your reading.

14. Practice walking to the front of an imaginary audience, anchoring in one spot, planting your feet about hip width, pausing while taking a deep imperceptible breath, and then introducing the title, author, and illustrator of a picture book.

15. Repeat Exercise 13 but use a picture book with extensive text and/or text with sentences that start on the right-hand page and end on the next page. Follow the instructions on Page 37 to determine how to make eye contact when reading an extended text.

Culminating Activity

Thoroughly prepare a picture book for reading aloud and then perform it for an appropriate live audience.

3

Reading Aloud
Chapter Books

The term *chapter book* in the context of this text refers to books that rely primarily on the print to communicate their messages. The amount of print may be limited or extensive, but there are few, if any, illustrations, and whatever illustrations exist are more decorative than essential. Thus, chapter books are typically read aloud with no need to share the illustrations with the audience. These books are usually much smaller in format than the typical picture book and are frequently divided into sections or chapters—thus the name *chapter book*. *The Midwife's Apprentice* (Cushman, 1995) is an example of a chapter book that has no illustration internal to the text, whereas *Charlotte's Web* (White, 1952) is an example of one that does. These two examples are fictional in content, but chapter books can be nonfiction as well, as is the case with *Hard Time: A Real Life Look at Juvenile Crime and Violence* (Bode & Mack, 1996). There are a few books with limited text which is not divided into sections, yet where the print is the primary means by which the messages in the books are communicated (e.g., Coatsworth's [1930] *The Cat Who Went To Heaven*, Mathis' [1975] *The Hundred Penny Box*, or Kennedy's [1979] *Inside My Feet*). I include these books and ones like them as chapter books as well.

Chapter books are primarily intended for older children who have developed fairly mature independent reading skills. However, some books in this category can be read aloud to young children assuming that the content is relevant to their lives.

SELECTION

The process of selecting chapter books to read aloud is generally the same as for picture books and involves developing a repertoire of read-aloud books and then selecting from that repertoire specific texts to be read on specific occasions.

Selection to Augment One's Repertoire

In general, the guidelines to be followed in building your repertoire of read-aloud chapter books are the same as for picture books: choosing texts you find personally meaningful and enjoyable and varying the choices across genre and readability level. In the later case, you can generally determine the readability by noting the book's format. The greater the amount of print and number of words per page, the smaller the size of the print, and the greater the complexity of the sentences, the older the intended reader.

The issue of the literary quality of the books you select into your repertoire is a bit more problematic with chapter books than with picture books. The problem involves the relative length of time it takes to read a book in its entirety. Obviously it takes much more time to complete a chapter book than it does to complete a typical picture book. Given the many demands on teachers and the limited amount of time school librarians have to spend with children, for example, the choice of what chapter books to read aloud completely in these settings becomes critical. Here it is probably best to consider only those texts of high literary quality so as to extend the literary horizons of your audience. Books chosen to read completely in school classrooms and libraries, for example, should be ones that are relevant to the students' current needs and interests. They should also be ones that are rich in language, thematic depth, and significance and are unique literarily as opposed to ones that are merely action packed and fast paced yet relatively meaningless or superficial and commonplace stylistically. If you feel that you aren't qualified to determine the literary quality of a book, you might want to access reviews of children's books through the use of two sources, *Book Review Digest* or *Book Review Index*, available at your library (see "Resources" at the end of the chapter).

Are there chapter books that shouldn't be read aloud? Yes, but the decision to exclude a particular book from your repertoire is a personal one and depends primarily on your judgment as to whether you can handle the complexity or uniqueness of the text and deliver it to an audience in a fluid, meaningful fashion. Recognize, however, that you may not be able to make this judgment until your have worked with the text a while in preparing to read it aloud.

Selection for a Specific Program

As was the case with picture books, selection of read-aloud chapter books involves, in part, matching the text with the needs, interests, and capabilities of the specific audience to be read to. The "Plot Concept, Theme–Trait Matching Process" introduced in chapter 2 can be used in selecting chapter books just as handily as with picture books. For example, middle-school teachers might justify their reading of *The Sign of the Beaver* (Speare, 1983) to their students as a result of the following analysis (see Example 3.1).

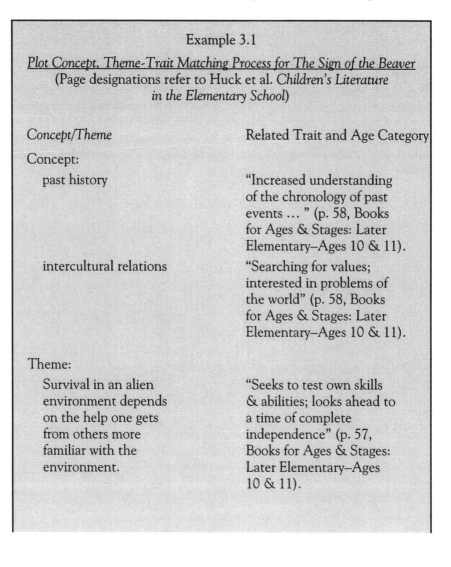

Example 3.1

Plot Concept, Theme-Trait Matching Process for The Sign of the Beaver
(Page designations refer to Huck et al. *Children's Literature in the Elementary School*)

Concept/Theme	Related Trait and Age Category
Concept:	
past history	"Increased understanding of the chronology of past events … " (p. 58, Books for Ages & Stages: Later Elementary–Ages 10 & 11).
intercultural relations	"Searching for values; interested in problems of the world" (p. 58, Books for Ages & Stages: Later Elementary–Ages 10 & 11).
Theme:	
Survival in an alien environment depends on the help one gets from others more familiar with the environment.	"Seeks to test own skills & abilities; looks ahead to a time of complete independence" (p. 57, Books for Ages & Stages: Later Elementary–Ages 10 & 11).

| We can learn important lessons about life from all cultures. | "Increased understanding of the chronology of past events.... Begins to see many dimensions of a problem" (p. 58, Books for Ages & Stages: Later Elementary–Ages 10 & 11). "Searching for values; interested in problems of the world. Can deal with abstract relationships; becoming more analytical" (p. 58, Books for Ages & Stages: Later Elementary–Ages 10 &11). |

Selection for a specific performance also involves determining the purpose of your reading. In general, there are two distinct purposes for reading chapter books to an audience. As implied earlier, you might choose to read a book in its entirety primarily for the purpose of extending the literary horizons of your audience or providing them with a literary experience that engenders a significant personal response on their part. School librarians might choose to read one of the Ramona stories such as *Ramona Forever* (Cleary, 1984) to primary grade students who might not yet have the capability to read the texts themselves but are developing an awareness of one of the major motifs in these books—the unsettling reality that adults are fallible. Seventh-grade teachers might choose to read *Dangerous Skies* (Staples, 1996) to their students to help them appreciate an author's use of extended metaphor in fiction (e.g., the use of stormy, springtime weather to underscore the turbulent events in this murder mystery) or to foster discussion regarding the importance of trust in the relationships one has with friends, parents, and authority figures in society.

There is a second, distinct purpose for reading aloud from a chapter book that involves sharing only a segment of a complete text with an audience. For example, your intention might be to read a small portion of a book to entice the audience members to read the book for themselves. This reading aloud would be one of a variety of techniques that could be used in presenting a book talk for children (Huck et al., 1997, p. 637). You might also use a brief excerpt from a book to define or exemplify some concept you wish to introduce to your audience. In *Mrs. Frisby and the Rats of NIMH* (O'Brien, 1972), for example, the concept of *rat race* can be exposed by reading pages 168 to 170.

Selecting an Excerpt for a Book Talk

In those instances where your intention is simply to motivate someone to read a book, attention to the literary quality of the books isn't as critical as when you have chosen to read a book in its entirety. In fact, if your intention here is to entice reluctant readers to read independently and recreationally, you may find the need to sacrifice some literary quality to ensure that the students can handle with relative ease the text you're promoting. What is more important in making your selections here is that you choose excerpts that are brief (keep the reading to 2 minutes or less) and high-powered. Choose excerpts that are either humorous, action-packed or adventurous, mysterious, suspenseful, or of intense interest to your audience. Consider reading a segment that ends in a cliffhanger where your audience will be curious to find out "what will happen next" but will have to read the book for themselves to find out. A short, hard-hitting presentation is far more effective in promoting a book than a longer one that is overly descriptive or detailed.

Frequently, the first chapter of a book or even the first few paragraphs is a good choice because authors know the importance of immediately capturing their readers' attention. Such is the case with the opening to Robinson's (1972) *The Best Christmas Pageant Ever*.

> The Herdmans were absolutely the worst kids in the history of the world. They lied and stole and smoked cigars (even the girls) and talked dirty and hit little kids and cussed their teachers and took the name of the Lord in vain and set fire to Fred Shoemaker's old broken-down toolhouse.

However, you may want to choose an excerpt from farther into the book perhaps as a means to convince your audience that the book is interesting throughout and not just at the beginning. For example, you might choose the fourth chapter in Robinson's book because of the humorous events that take place when the Herdmans attend the first rehearsal for the upcoming Christmas pageant. Or you might choose the 15th chapter of Speare's (1983) *The Sign of the Beaver* because of the suspenseful nature surrounding the main characters being attacked by a bear. Then, too, a good choice to pique the curiosity of third or fourth graders might be chapter 4 from

Rockwell's (1973) *How to Eat Fried Worms* where Billy, the main character, first experiences eating a live worm—a gross but interesting prospect for many third and fourth graders.

Pay attention to the ends of chapters or other sections of a book where cliffhangers are likely to occur. These segments serve as natural choices to read during book talks because they leave audience members with a sense of incompleteness and suspense that can only be satisfied by their reading the book themselves. Note too that cliffhangers are used in all genres of literature, not just suspense thrillers where you would naturally expect them to occur. Reading the end of the first chapter of Cooney's (1997) *The Terrorist* which ends with the sentence, "The package exploded," would be an obvious and good choice but so would the reading of chapter 6 of the fantasy *Ella Enchanted* (Levine, 1997), which ends:

> Against my will I took a step. I stopped, and the trembling started again. Another step. And another. I saw nothing, except that leering face, looming closer and closer.

Book Format

The format of the chapter book you choose to read from must also be considered in the selection process. Chapter books come in basically two formats: hardback and paperback. Each has its own unique advantages and disadvantages with regard to reading aloud performance.

A hardback is typically a bit larger and the print a bit larger than with its paperback counterpart. This makes viewing the text of a hardback a bit easier on the eyes. The pages of a hardback are usually of better quality paper than in paperbacks, which makes page turning easier and the pages less likely to tear or become detached at the gutter. Hardbacks are also more firmly bound than a paperback, which means that they will hold together longer and be more valuable to you if you intend to read from these copies for years to come.

Paperbacks are much lighter than hardbacks, more portable, and a bit easier to hold up when reading for any extended period of time, and they are less expensive than hardbacks. In addition, if you must mark up a book with performance notes (see Preparation), you might feel more comfortable taking a pencil or pen to a paperback rather than a hardback. Then, too, it's less expensive to have multiple copies of a paperback available for students to read themselves so that teachers and librarians who read aloud in book talks might choose the paperback to read from. This allows students to make an immediate connection between the performance text and the multiple texts displayed in a nearby reading center or on a library cart.

PREPARATION

The need for careful preparation is no less important when reading aloud a chapter book than when reading aloud a picture book. As was mentioned with picture books, the quality of preparation determines the quality of the performance and transforms the mere reciting of lines in a text into an art form.

Because the illustrations typically aren't shown to the audience when reading a chapter book, book handling and movement aren't a problem here as was the case with picture books. Nonetheless, decisions must be made well in advance of the reading of chapter books regarding the articulation of unusual words, lengthy or awkward phrases and sentences (or ones that extend from one page to another), as well as decisions about phrasing, placing emphasis on specific words or phrases, pausing, or altering the pacing of the reading. Viewing the text and page turning is typically more problematic in reading chapter books than with picture books due to the reduced size of the print, the increased amount of print per page, and the relative thinness of the pages. However, you will be directly facing the text you are reading from so there is some compensation for these format problems. Eye contact with your audience does become a bit more difficult (although no less critical) due to the increase in the amount of text to be processed by the performer.

Moreover, there is a greater likelihood that you will need to skip over significant portions of text (oftentimes skipping clumps of pages at a time) particularly when reading aloud during a book talk. As such, editing decisions will have to be made and you will have to practice skipping from one part of a book to the next part without any significant interruption in the flow of the reading. Then, too, if you are reading only an excerpt and the excerpt starts beyond the first few pages of a book, you will likely have to provide an introduction to the segment to be read and, depending on your purpose for reading, some follow-up remarks to finish off the performance.

Given all that has been said, two things must be analyzed when preparing for a chapter book performance: the text and oneself.

Analysis of Text

When reading a book in its entirety, thoroughly analyze the text prior to your first performance and consider setting aside a copy of the book exclusively as your read-aloud copy. In this copy, then, you can mark up the text with performance notes based on your analysis and subsequent decisions you've made as to how to orally interpret the text. Because your interpretation may change with repeated performances of the text, it seems wise to use a pencil rather than a pen to do the marking so that changing the notes is possible.

Marking a book with performance notes is an important step in the preparation of any chapter book to be read aloud but takes on added importance with a book that you will read in its entirety. If you intend to read the book on more than one occasion—a likely prospect because you will have put much thought and time into the analysis of a lengthy text—you want to avoid having to reanalyze the text prior to performances subsequent to the first. Keeping performance notes in a separate read-aloud copy of the book enables you to avoid this reanalysis, yet provides you with interpretive information that can quickly be reviewed prior to the subsequent performances—a good way to cut down on the time it takes to prepare for these subsequent performances

Creating Performance Notes

Utilizing the selection criteria provided earlier, the preparation process actually begins by determining whether the book is to be read in its entirety and, in the case of reading only an excerpt, choosing which segment to read from a text. Once chosen, begin the analytical process by determining whether there is a need to alter the text in any way. As a general rule, if you are reading a text in its entirety, it is best not to edit the text at all, thus respecting the literary effort of the author. If, however, your intent is to read only an excerpt, it may be necessary to edit the text to meet your specific purpose. Don't worry that you're undermining the essential literary quality of the text in doing this editing. In enticing the audience members to read the book for themselves or in using an excerpt to exemplify some concept, your purpose here is wholly different than authentically representing the book. Editing the text may be vital in meeting your stated purpose.

When you have chosen the text to be read, the process is similar to that involved in analyzing the text of a picture book. First read the text silently several times; then read it out loud to determine what problems you may have with articulation or flow. Use the list of questions raised on page 22 of chapter 2 to aid in your analysis. Consider as well changes in the mood and pace of stories you are reading, and think about places where pausing would

---

Figure 3.1

Sample Performance Note Symbols

Underline: Add special emphasis to the word or phrase.

/: Pause briefly.

//: Pause for a moderate length of time.

///: Stop reading.

Quotation Marks: Denotes text that reads like a quote, monologue, or dialogue but which isn't marked as such in the original text.

Arrow under text: Continue reading; don't interrupt the flow (appears most frequently when a sentence is divided over two pages).

Arrow from one textual unit to another: Indicates that a substantial amount of text is to be skipped; the arrow directs the reader's eye to the text to be read.

Words crossed out: Indicates a small unit of text to be skipped.

Words crossed out with other words written over the top: Indicates a word substitution.

Parenthesis around a word or phrase: read in a parenthetic tone of voice.

Marginal notes:

   "Start": Indicates where to start the reading (used when reading an excerpt)

   "Ph": Look for a word, phrase, sentence that is difficult to articulate (the difficult unit may be underlined).

   "Slow": Slow the pace of the reading.

   "Speed": Speed up the pace of the reading.

   Specific words/phrases such as "underplay," "whisper," "yell," "surprise," etc. : specific directions for interpreting the text in a specific spot. This will often involve dialogue.

---

add a dramatic touch to your performance. When you begin to make decisions regarding your oral interpretation of the text, you will want to begin marking your read-aloud copy using a set of symbols that make obvious and immediate sense to you. See Fig. 3.1 for a sample set of symbols that I use, but feel free to choose your own.

Sample Text Analysis When Reading a Book in Its Entirety

As an example of this process, consider chapter 5 of *The Sign of the Beaver* (Speare, 1983). First, look at the chapter as if you were reading the entire book to an audience (in this text, Pages 22 and 23 face one another as do Pages 24 and 25). Your marked-up copy might look like the following:

Chapter 5

Day after day he kept remembering the bee tree.

He and his father had discovered it weeks ago. High in

a tree, at the swampy edge of the pond they had called

Ph Loon Pond, the bees were buzzing in and out of an old

woodpecker hole. Matt had thought they were wild

bees, but his father said no, there were no bees at all in

America till the colonists brought them from England.

This swarm must have escaped from one of the river

towns. Bees were better left alone, Pa said.

Matt He felt he could scarcely endure another meal of

plain fish. He was hungry for a bit of something tasty.

Knowing so well his fondness for molasses, his mother

had persuaded them to carry that little keg all the way to

Ph Maine when his father would rather have gone without.

She would have smiled to see him running his finger

round and round the empty keg like a child and licking

off the last drop the bear had missed. Now he couldn't

stop thinking about that honey. It would be worth a

sting or two just to have a taste of it. There couldn't be

much danger in going up that tree and taking just a

little a cupful perhaps that the bees would never miss.

One morning he made up his mind to try it, come what

Ph might.

22

It was an easy tree to climb, with branches as neatly placed as the rungs of a ladder. The bees did not seem to notice as he pulled himself higher and higher. Even when his head was on a level with the hole, they flew lazily in and out, not paying him any mind. The hole was small, not big enough for his hand and the spoon he had brought with him. Peering in, he could just glimpse, (far inside) the golden mass of honeycomb. The bark all around the hole was rotted and crumbling. Cautiously he put his fingers on the edge and gave a slight tug. A good-sized piece of bark broke off into his hand.

speed   With it came the bees. With a furious buzzing they came pouring from the broken hole. The humming grew to a roar, like a great wind. Matt felt a sharp pain on his neck, then another and another. The angry creatures swarmed along his hands and bare arms, in his hair, on *and* his face.

How he got down out of that tree he never remembered. Water! If he could reach water he could escape them. Bellowing and waving his arms, he plunged toward the pond. The bees were all around him. He could not see through the whirling cloud of them. The boggy ground sucked at his feet. He pulled one foot clear out of his boot, went stumbling over sharp roots to the water's edge, and flung himself forward. His foot caught in a fallen branch and he wrenched it clear. Dazed with pain, he sank down into the icy shelter of the water.

He came up choking. Just above the water the angry bees circled. Twice more he ducked his head and held it down till his lungs were bursting. He tried to swim

23

out into the pond but his feet were tangled in dragging
weeds. When he tried to jerk them free, a fierce pain
ran up his leg and he went under again, thrashing his
arms wildly.

Then something lifted him. His head came up from
the water and he gulped air into his aching lungs.
He felt strong arms around him. Half conscious, he
dreamed that his father was carrying him, and he did
not wonder how this could be. Presently he knew he
was lying on dry ground. Though his eyelids were
swollen almost shut, he could see two figures bending
over him—unreal, half-naked figures with dark faces.
Then, as his wits began to return to him, he saw that
they were Indians, an old man and a boy. The man's
hands were reaching for his throat, and in panic Matt
tried to jerk away.

"Not move," a deep voice ordered. "Bee needles have
poison. Must get out."

Matt was too weak to struggle. He could not even lift
his head. Now that he was out of the cold water, his
skin seemed to be on fire from head to toe, yet he could
not stop shivering. He had to lie helpless while the
man's hands moved over his face and neck and body.
Gradually he realized that they were gentle hands,
probing and rubbing at one tender spot after another.
His panic began to die away.

He could still not think clearly. Things seemed to
keep fading before he could quite grasp them. He could
not protest when the man lifted him again and carried
him like a baby. It did not seem to matter where they
were taking him, but shortly he found himself lying on

24

his own bed in his own cabin. He was alone; the Indians
had gone. He lay, too tired and sore to figure out how
he came to be there, knowing only that the nightmare
of whirling bees and choking water was past and that
he was safe. ||

Some time passed. Then once again the Indian was
bending over him, holding a wooden spoon against his
lips. He swallowed in spite of himself, even when he
found it was not food, but some bitter medicine. He
was left alone again, and presently he slept. |||

25

As was suggested when reading an entire text, any alterations are kept to
a minimum; only two small ones in this case. In the beginning of the second
paragraph on Page 22, I have chosen to substitute *Matt* for *He* because, without the change, the audience might erroneously assume that *He* refers to
Matt's father, who was the subject of the previous sentence. The second
change involves the addition of the word *and* between *hair* and *on* at the end
of the second paragraph on Page 23. Its addition makes the reading of the
sentence it has been added to more natural for me.

The text of the paperback copy is relatively easy to read. There are no major problems with print size or unusual text placement. However, there are
several instances where the flow of the reading might be interrupted unless
care is taken to avoid this problem. There is a page turn from Page 23 to Page
24 that divides a sentence that must be read quickly with no interruption.
On Page 24 in the first full paragraph, the comma that separates the words
unreal and *half-naked* can be misinterpreted as a period (the syntax in the
sentence leading up to this point could also lead to this misinterpretation),
thus causing the reader to end the sentence here instead of continuing the
flow as is truly intended.

Similarly, in the seventh sentence of the third paragraph on Page 23, I
tend to want to violate the true syntax here by ending the sentence after the
word *clear* (as in "He pulled one foot clear. Then ... ") probably because
Speare has written this scene primarily using short, staccato sentences.
Moreover, maintaining the naturally rapid pace of the story as you finish the
third paragraph and begin the fourth paragraph on Page 23 requires contin-

uing the flow of the reading as you read from one paragraph to the next. The same situation exists on Page 24 between the first two paragraphs. In all these instances, the arrow drawn beneath the text is a signal to avoid any pausing.

There are several spots in the text that can cause articulation problems. Most problems of this nature will usually be idiosyncratic, thus differing from one person to the next. On Page 22, I tend to want to say *Long* instead of *Loon*, *cup* instead of *cupful*, and *may* instead of *might*. On Page 24, I want to reverse the words *could* and *still* in the first sentence of the last paragraph. These spots may be a problem for me, they may not be of concern to others. Sometimes, however, the syntax or complexity of a sentence may not be commonplace and, therefore, cause most folks problems. Such is the case with the sentence that begins, "Knowing so well his fondness for molasses ... " in the second paragraph on Page 22, the phrase " ... were tangled in dragging weeds" on Page 24, and the dialectical sentences "Not move. Bee needles have poison, Must get out," also on Page 24. As such, I have flagged these problem spots by placing "Ph" (meaning "Phrasing") in the nearby margin to remind myself to practice pronouncing these sections before each performance and then taking care in reading them during a performance.

Note one other problem that is created by syntax. On Page 24, look carefully at the sentence, "'Not move,' a deep voice ordered." In normal oral language, the two major parts of this sentence would probably be spoken in the reverse order—that is, "A deep voice ordered, 'Not move.'" If this were the order of the sentence to be read aloud in the text, the reader would know how to orally interpret "Not move." That is, read "Not move" as a sharp command with a deep voice. But as is often the case in print literature, the interpretive words follow the text to be interpreted. Thus, I have written the words *Deep Command* in the margin to remind me beforehand how to read "Not move."

An additional format problem is created on Page 22 in the fourth sentence of the first paragraph. The words " ... no, there were no bees at all in America till the colonists brought them from England" form a quote from Matt's father, but are not identified as such in this text by the use of quotation marks. Therefore, to help me read these words as a quote using the appropriate intonation, I have penciled in quotation marks. Similarly, the words *far inside* close to the end of the first paragraph on Page 23 seem parenthetic to me. As a reminder to read them that way, I have bracketed them with parentheses.

As a final step in the text analysis, consider the pacing of the story. The chapter begins at a moderate pace simply describing Matt's desire to add variation to his current diet. Even as Matt climbs the tree to retrieve some honey, we note the leisurely pace as exemplified on Page 23 by the bees *lazily* coming and going. But the pace changes in an instant when Matt breaks a piece of bark from the tree. It becomes *furious* and continues at a high rate of speed throughout Matt's efforts to escape the angry bees then settles back down to a moderate pace again on Page 24 when Matt feels strong arms surrounding him. Incorporating these changes in pace can be aided by writing the marginal notes *speed* where the pace quickens and *slow down* where it settles back to a moderate pace.

Pace is also affected by pausing in the text, and there are several spots in this chapter where pausing seems either natural or necessary for dramatic emphasis. These spots are marked with a single or double slash (depending on the length of the pause) and occur in a number of places. On Page 22, for example, I pause after *Now* in the second paragraph because I feel Speare wants this time word to be the focus of the sentence. Also, in that same paragraph, to avoid my personal tendency to ignore the dash after *little*, I have inserted a slash. Where major pace changes (after *lungs* in the first full paragraph on Page 24) or time/scene changes occur (between the last two paragraphs in the chapter), it is important to pause for a moderate length of time. Thus, a double slash is used in these instances. Note that these changes don't always happen at the end of paragraphs, as is the case on Page 24.

Sample Text Analysis When Reading an Excerpt

Now, by contrast, assume you are going to use chapter 5 for a book talk where your intent is to entice the audience to read the book themselves. The following is how the markings might appear in this instance.

When reading an excerpt, the first decision involves choosing to read only the text that serves your purpose. In keeping the reading brief, hard-hitting, and enticing, I have chosen not to read a large portion of the chapter, focusing only on those parts that relate to Matt's desire to get some honey and his suspenseful encounter with the bees. Thus, on Page 22, there is no need to read of Matt's thoughts about where these bees have come from in the first paragraph or his mother's persuasive efforts in the second paragraph. A line has been drawn through the affected sentences denoting that they shouldn't be read. Also, I have decided to end the reading in cliffhanger fashion by stopping at the end of the first paragraph on Page 24 (denoted by use of a triple slash) when Matt's fate is very uncertain. The remainder of the chapter, then, is left unread.

In this example, it was necessary to skip over only limited amounts of text. If you should ever have a need to skip over several pages of text, con-

Chapter 5

Day after day he kept remembering the bee tree.
He and his father had discovered it weeks ago. High in
a tree, at the swampy edge of the pond they had called
Loon Pond, the bees were buzzing in and out of an old
woodpecker hole. ~~Matt had thought they were wild~~
~~bees, but his father said no, there were no bees at all in~~
~~America till the colonists brought them from England.~~
~~This swarm must have escaped from one of the river~~
~~towns. Bees were better left alone, Pa said.~~

He felt he could scarcely endure another meal of
plain fish. He was hungry for a bit of something tasty.
~~Knowing so well his fondness for molasses, his mother~~
~~had persuaded them to carry that little keg all the way to~~
~~Maine when his father would rather have gone without.~~
~~She would have smiled to see him running his finger~~
~~round and round the empty keg like a child and licking~~
~~off the last drop the bear had missed.~~ Now he couldn't
stop thinking about that honey. It would be worth a
sting or two just to have a taste of it. There couldn't be
much danger in going up that tree and taking just a
little a cupful perhaps that the bees would never miss.
One morning he made up his mind to try it, come what
might.

22

It was an easy tree to climb, with branches as neatly placed as the rungs of a ladder. The bees did not seem to notice as he pulled himself higher and higher. Even when his head was on a level with the hole, they flew lazily in and out, not paying him any mind. The hole was small, not big enough for his hand and the spoon he had brought with him. Peering in, he could just glimpse, (far inside,) the golden mass of honeycomb. The bark all around the hole was rotted and crumbling. Cautiously he put his fingers on the edge and gave a slight tug. A good-sized piece of bark broke off into his hand.

Speed

With it came the bees. With a furious buzzing they came pouring from the broken hole. The humming grew to a roar, like a great wind. Matt felt a sharp pain on his neck, then another and another. The angry creatures swarmed along his hands and bare arms, in his hair, on *and* his face.

How he got down out of that tree he never remembered. Water! If he could reach water he could escape them. Bellowing and waving his arms, he plunged toward the pond. The bees were all around him. He could not see through the whirling cloud of them. The boggy ground sucked at his feet. He pulled one foot clear out of his boot, went stumbling over sharp roots to the water's edge, and flung himself forward. His foot caught in a fallen branch and he wrenched it clear. Dazed with pain, he sank down into the icy shelter of the water.

He came up choking. Just above the water the angry bees circled. Twice more he ducked his head and held it down till his lungs were bursting. He tried to swim

23

out into the pod but his feet were tangled in dragging / Ph
weeds. When he tried to jerk them free, a fierce pain
ran up his leg and he went under again, thrashing his
arms wildly. ///

Then something lifted him. His head came up from
the water and he gulped air into his aching lungs.
He felt strong arms around him. Half conscious, he
dreamed that his father was carrying him, and he did
not wonder how this could be. Presently he knew he
was lying on dry ground. Though his eyelids were
swollen almost shut, he could see two figures bending
over him—unreal, half-naked figures with dark faces.
Then, as his wits began to return to him, he saw that
they were Indians, an old man and a boy. The man's
hands were reaching for his throat, and in panic Matt
tried to jerk away.

"Not move," a deep voice ordered. "Bee needles have
poison. Must get out."

Matt was too weak to struggle. He could not even lift
his head. Now that he was out of the cold water, his
skin seemed to be on fire from head to toe, yet he could
not stop shivering. He had to lie helpless while the
man's hands moved over his face and neck and body.
Gradually he realized that they were gentle hands,
probing and rubbing at one tender spot after another.
His panic began to die away.

He could still not think clearly. Things seemed to
keep fading before he could quite grasp them. He could
not protest when the man lifted him again and carried
him like a baby. It did not seem to matter where they
were taking him, but shortly he found himself lying on

24

his own bed in his own cabin. He was alone; the Indians

had gone. He lay, too tired and sore to figure out how

he came to be there, knowing only that the nightmare

of whirling bees and choking water was past and that

he was safe.

Some time passed. Then once again the Indian was

bending over him, holding a wooden spoon against his

lips. He swallowed in spite of himself, even when

he found it was not food, but some bitter medicine. He

was left alone again, and presently he slept.

25

sider using a paper clip to clump the unused pages together. By placing the clip on the upper right edge of the clipped pages, you will be able to turn to the next spot to be read quickly and efficiently.

In making these dramatic cuts, it seemed to me that the natural sequence of the intact text was significantly affected. Moreover, in reading the chosen excerpt, it seemed more natural to first reveal Matt's desire to spice up his diet before introducing the bee tree and, subsequently, Matt's decision to get honey from the tree. As such, when reading this excerpt, I have altered the original sequence in the text. Note that I have chosen to start the reading with the second paragraph on Page 22 rather than the first (substituting the word *Matt* for *He*). After this first sentence, I then read the first three sentences in the first paragraph followed by the last four sentences in the second paragraph (again substituting *Matt* for *Now he*). Note the use of arrows to direct my attention to this sequence. Continuing onto Page 23 and the top of Page 24, I keep the sequence as Speare has written it.

Beyond these changes, the decisions I have made regarding the reading of the excerpt are the same as those I made when reading the entire chapter. As such, the performance notes remain the same as before.

One other tip. For ease in locating the start of the excerpt, attach a post-it note upside down on the first page of the excerpt with its edge protruding from the top of the book. By placing your fingers on the exposed edge of the note and sliding them down into the closed book, you will be able to locate the starting page with ease.

Preparing an Introduction and Follow-up

When reading an excerpt other than the first chapter in a book, it is neces-sary to prepare an introduction and follow-up to the segment being read. Remember that the text you'll read has been pulled out of context. Compre-hension of the excerpt assumes an understanding of the prior context. Thus, you must provide the audience with just enough information from that prior context to enable them to understand the segment you are reading. Then, too, you'll want to provide your listeners with some reason for listening. Both notions can be dealt with in an introduction, but you want to keep your introductory comments as brief as possible. Try keeping it to less than a min-ute; the briefer the better.

To create an appropriate introduction, review the excerpt and generate a list of questions that must be answered in order to make the excerpt mean-ingful when read out of the context of the whole story. Then find answers to the questions. Having previously determined your purpose for reading the excerpt during the selection process, you can now begin to create an intro-duction. Using the sample excerpt from *The Sign of the Beaver*, where the purpose is to encourage personal reading by the audience, the following is a list of questions from the targeted excerpt:

Who is Matt?
Where and when does this story take place?
Matt appears to be on his own. How did this happen
    and what bearing has it on his desire to get
    the honey?
Why couldn't Matt's father (mentioned early in the
    excerpt) have helped him avoid the disaster
    with the bees?
What circumstances have caused Matt to crave
    honey/need some variety in his diet?

In responding to these questions, it isn't necessary to go into great detail, literally retelling the entire story to this point in the book. Craft an introduc-tion to provide just enough information to render the excerpt meaningful. From chapters 1 to 4, we know the following:

Matt is 12, nearly 13, years old. It is the summer of 1768. Matt and his father have come to the Maine wilderness and built a log cabin that will be his fam-ily's new home. Father has just returned to Massachusetts to bring the re-mainder of the family to Maine leaving Matt alone to protect the log cabin. Father predicts that he will be able to return to Maine in 6 weeks. Matt's supply of food is eaten by a marauding bear and his rifle, used primarily to hunt for meat, is stolen by a vagrant woodsman. For several days, all that Matt has had to eat is the fish he is able to catch in a nearby stream.

From these data, it is possible to create an introduction such as the following:

> *The Sign of the Beaver* by Elizabeth George Speare would be a good book for those of you who like adventure stories. The main character is Matt, a twelve year old, and the story takes place in the summer of 1768 in the wilderness that is now the State of Maine. Matt and his father have built a log cabin on some land they own but Matt's father has returned to Massachusetts to bring the rest of the family back to the cabin that will be the family's new home. This trip will take about 6 weeks so Matt is left alone to protect the cabin. But during the first several weeks Matt becomes careless. His rifle which he uses primarily to hunt for meat, is stolen by a vagrant woodsman, and a bear gets inside the cabin and eats all of Matt's food supplies. So for some days, Matt has only eaten the fish he is able to catch from a nearby pond. Here we pick up the story.... (55 seconds)

Feel free to vary the introduction from time to time (variation will happen naturally anyway). For example, if your students have read other books by Speare, or have read *Robinson Crusoe*, which is referred to in later chapters, you can remind them of that before introducing this book. You might want to write your introduction on an index card and tuck it inside your read-aloud copy for handy reference before later performances. Avoid reading the introduction from the card in performance, and don't memorize it word for word. Simply practice telling the introduction informally, letting it vary naturally from one performance to the next. When you are able to deliver the introduction fluidly, note the average time it takes to deliver it and record this information on your index card. This information will come in handy when planning a performance.

It is typically necessary to follow the reading with some sort of concluding statement but keep your remarks brief because any follow-up is anticlimactic to the reading. For a book talk excerpt, consider presenting an interesting challenge to the audience In the case of the excerpt from *The Sign of the Beaver*, the following might be a good way to conclude the performance:

> Will Matt survive this crisis? Read Speare's *The Sign of the Beaver* and find out for yourself.

Whatever you say to conclude the performance, always be sure to mention the title of the story and the author in your follow-up. Also consider recording your follow-up on the index card where you have written your introduction. Timing the follow-up won't be necessary because it will be quite brief.

Analysis of Self

Review the questions listed on Page 35of chapter 2 and the suggestions on subsequent pages in that chapter. In general, these questions and suggestions are as applicable in preparing to read a chapter book as they are in preparing for a picture book reading.

There are, however, some singular issues that require special mention. First, when reading a chapter book, the attention of the audience is naturally on you rather than the book, as was the case with picture books. Keeping this in mind, then, you want to begin the performance by anchoring yourself at the midpoint in front of your audience and directly facing them. Keeping your head up as well as the book, project your voice out over the book toward the audience, but avoid blocking the view of anyone in the audience with the book. As always, engage in as much eye contact with your audience as possible. Note that, because you will typically have more text and smaller print to process in a chapter book as compared to a picture book, maintaining maximum eye contact may be more difficult here. However, because the book is just under your line of vision with your audience, getting your eyes out of the book and on your audience involves less head and eye movement than was the case with picture book reading. The tricky part here is to avoid loosing your place when your eyes return to the book. If this is a problem for you, hold the book with both hands and run the thumb of one of them down the margin next to the line of print as you read, stopping when you make eye contact. Your thumb will serve as a general marker of the spot your eyes are to return to when refocusing on the text.

Putting It All Together

If your preparation has been thorough, you will have developed much confidence in your ability to read chapter books aloud. All that remains is to practice what you have planned. But practice is no less important in the performance of chapter books than it is with picture books. Reading the text fluidly as you have planned it while maintaining good eye contact takes some effort on your part. As before, the practice must be out loud. Once you have established fluidity and are interpreting the text in accordance with your performance notes, you may want to augment the practicing by envisioning an imaginary audience in front of you. In this way, you can focus attention specifically on practicing making eye contact, thus extending to the maximum your direct contact with the audience.

Be sure to time several readings once good flow is established, and note the average time it takes you to read the text. I find it helpful in planning a performance to note the time right on the text, usually at the beginning of each chapter or excerpt to be read.

As an additional suggestion, consider creating a collection of copies of your favorite read-aloud texts to be used exclusively for that purpose and shelve them together in a single spot in your personal library.

Avoid reading the introduction from a card or reciting it word for word. Just know what information you have to present and deliver it in an informal, relaxed fashion while making direct eye contact with all the members of your audience. This is a marvelous opportunity to connect with your audience.

As with picture books, you may want to record information about your read-aloud chapter books. A sample form follows (see Fig. 3.2).

Figure 3.2

Read Aloud Chapter Book

Book Title:_____

Author/Illustrator:_____

Publisher/Date of Publication:_____

Location of Book:_____

Average Time to Read Book/Chapter/Excerpt:_____

Intended Audience:_____

Rationale (Employ Plot Concept, Theme-Trait Matching Process):

Personal Appeal (State why the book interests you
        personally beyond any utilitarian value):

Story Preparation (List potential problems and solutions in each area):

Text Analysis:

Self-Analysis:

Introduction(s):

DELIVERY

Confidence in reading chapter books aloud is established when selection and preparation have been thorough. The most important thing to remember during the delivery, then, is to relax and enjoy the performance because, in this way, you will be able to maximize the interpretive decisions you have made and practiced beforehand.

What to Do Prior to Delivery

Audience arrangement isn't as critical in reading chapter books as it is with picture books because there are no illustrations to be seen. Still, if you feel that certain members of the audience aren't comfortable or are likely to interfere with the performance, do some rearranging if it is possible, but do it before you begin the performance. If no such rearrangement is necessary and your audience is settled in to listen to you as you make your entrance, simply remember to anchor in one spot and pause before you begin while making eye contact with everyone in front of you.

What to Do During the Delivery

Your best bet for controlling the actions and reactions of your audience during the performance is through eye contact and knowing your text so well that you will be able to predict any unusual audience behavior and not be taken by surprise. Still, completely unpredictable things may happen during a performance. Try dealing with them using the same suggestions mentioned in chapter 2. Also know that you are freer to move about when reading a chapter book because you don't have to worry about sharing any illustrations with the audience. Thus, if some disruptive behavior is happening in your audience, you can continue reading while moving close to the trouble spot, thus imposing proximity control on the disruptive individuals. You could even place a gentle hand on the shoulder of a disruptive person while continuing to attend to your reading.

What to Do After the Delivery

It is always good to reflect on a performance after it is over. While the performance is fresh in your mind, you may want to evaluate it and note (in writing if important enough) any unusual or serendipitous circumstances that occurred that will help you augment or improve your performance in the future.

EXTENDED PRACTICE ACTIVITIES

Developmental Activities

Choose from the following list of activities those that will help you improve your ability to read chapter books aloud. Work with a collection of books that you have selected from your personal library or a classroom, school, or public library.

1. Distinguish chapter books from picture books.

2. Looking only at the format of the books and utilizing the guidelines suggested on Page 44, approximate the age appropriateness of each book.

3. Identify the topical content for a sample book or two. By looking at the list of topics covered in a single book, is it possible for you to identify what age person might find this book interesting?

4. Using the directives in chapter 2 and a few sample books, identify some themes in each of the books.

5. Using the charts provided in the *Children's Literature in the Elementary School* (Huck et al., 1997, pp. 52–59) or in *Through the Eyes of a Child* (Norton, 1999, pp. 6–43) and some chapter books, employ the Plot Concept, Theme–Trait Matching Process to identify what age child the books would be appropriate for. You may want to begin by discussing concepts and themes for *Charlotte's Web, The Midwife's Apprentice,* or other pieces of fiction mentioned in this chapter.

6. Using chapter books you have read recently, determine which should be read to an audience in their entirety (ones that are of high literary quality) and those that would be better saved to read in a book talk. Refer to *Book Review Digest* or *Book Review Index* if you need to locate book reviews to help you judge the literary quality of a book.

7. As a follow-up to Activity 6, locate segments in the book talk books that would be ideal for using during a book talk. Use pp. 47–48 of this chapter to help you.

8. If you have both the hardback and paperback copies of the same books, examine them to determine which would be best to use as your read-aloud copy. See pp. 48–49 in this chapter for things to consider in making your choices.

9. Without reading the text of a book, simply practice turning its pages quickly so that you discover how best to do it. All the while, practice shifting your focus from the last word on one page to the first word on the next.

10. With the text from any chapter book, read it aloud with no preparation to discover what problems it presents regarding articulation and fluency. Then determine how you might solve the problems you encounter. Use the questions in chapter 2 to help you here.

11. Repeat Activity 10, but this time locate spots where it would be natural to vary the pace of the reading, pause for dramatic effect, or alter the volume, pitch, tone, or rhythm of your reading.

12. Now read aloud the book you've been working with in Activities 10 and 11 all the while practicing slow, smooth, and extensive eye contact with an imaginary audience seated beyond your book and then refocusing your eyes on the next appropriate spot in the text. Remember to keep the book and your head up and project your voice over the book. (Later, you can precede this exercise by practicing walking up before an audience to begin a performance. Remember to anchor yourself in one spot, then pause while making eye contact with all the members of the audience. Once done, then begin reading.)

13. Practice preparing an excerpt to be read in a book talk (e.g., use chap. 15 in Speare's *The Sign of the Beaver*) or one to be used to exemplify some concept (the concept of *rat race* using pp. 168–170 in O'Brien's *Mrs. Frisby and the Rats of NIMH*).

Culminating Activities

1. Thoroughly prepare an excerpt from a chapter book for reading in a book talk and then perform it for an appropriate live audience.

2. Thoroughly prepare an excerpt from a chapter book for reading as a means to exemplify some concept and then perform it for an appropriate live audience.

3. Thoroughly prepare an entire chapter book for reading and then perform it for an appropriate live audience.

RESOURCES

Book Review Digest. H. W. Wilson Company. (References a limited number of reviews of both fiction and nonfiction from a limited number of review journals. Each entry includes bibliographic information for each review listed, a brief summary of the reviewed book, and excerpts from a few critical reviews.)

Book Review Index. Gale Research Company. (References reviews to all books, fiction and nonfiction, that have been reviewed. Provides only bibliographic information for each review.)

4

Reading Poetry Aloud

Reading poetry aloud requires special consideration due to its uniqueness as a literary art form. It is a far more compact means of communication and relies more heavily on musical and metaphorical language than is the case with prose. Every word counts for so much more in a poem, and the messages communicated through poetry are typically presented in a far more condensed and lyrical form than in prose writing. As such, poetry is truly intended to be heard as well as seen particularly because of its lyrical quality. Unfortunately, poetry is not generally as appreciated as is prose. All the more reason to share poetry with audiences by reading it aloud with enthusiasm yet with a sensitivity to its uniqueness.

SELECTION

Because of its condensed nature, poetry can sometimes appear obscure; the meaning of a poem difficult to determine with any specificity. This obscurity is, in fact, a strength of the genre. A poem opens the possibility to multiple interpretations, thus capable of engaging each individual who experiences it in a very personal way. Yet this special quality also presents the performer with a problem. As has been stated before, when choosing to read literature aloud to an audience, it is essential that you enjoy what you are sharing. In turn, this means that you must bring some meaning to the literature you choose to read aloud. This single selection principle is all the more critical in choosing poetry because of its relatively obscure nature and the generally negative attitudes that people have toward it. You needn't worry so much that the audience will derive the same meaning from a poem as you do (they probably won't anyway). But unless you find the poem personally meaningful, it is unlikely that you will read it with any vitality, thus perpetuating the popular notion that poetry is a literary wasteland. As such, very special care must be taken in choosing poems for your read-aloud repertoire: Be certain to choose only those poems that make sense to you.

When choosing poetry for a specific performance, special care must also be taken particularly when reading to children. Several recent research reports have provided interesting insights into the poetry preferences of children, particularly when the medium of communication is reading aloud by an adult (Fisher & Natarella, 1982; Kutiper, 1985; Sebesta, 1983; Terry, 1974). In general, children prefer poetry that is humorous or narrative in nature, personally familiar or relevant, and more than less musical in form. By contrast, they tend to reject poetry that is overly descriptive, obscure, and dated or antiquated. The reason children seem to appreciate such a narrow range of poetry is because, as Norton (1999) stated: " ... adults infrequently share poetry with children" (p. 411). This research suggests that teachers and librarians reconsider what poetry they read aloud to children, choosing only those types of poems that children prefer. However, despite her own findings, Terry (1974. p. 55) suggested that educators make poetry available to children on an extensive basis and choose a wide variety of poems to share with them. In this way, it may be possible to extend the poetry interests of our children beyond the seemingly limited array of poetry they say they prefer.

Huck et al. (1997, p. 392) provided an additional caution when selecting poetry to read to children. She referred to Longfellow's "The Children's Hour," Whittier's "The Barefoot Boy" (Ferris, 1957, pp. 51, 544), and the poetry of Joan Walsh Anglund when recommending that adults avoid choosing poetry that is about children rather than for them. Poetry that provides a nostalgic, reminiscent, or overly sentimental view of childhood or verse that preaches to children, as does this poetry, is irrelevant and inappropriate for them.

One final problem with poetry in general involves the physical shape that some poems take. Much of the import of the following limerick (Peter Pauper Press, 1954) is lost unless an audience can actually see the poem:

> There was a young lady of Diss
> Who said, "Now I think skating bliss."
>   This no more will she skate,
>   For a wheel off her skate
>   siɥʇ ǝʞᴉl ƃuᴉɥʇǝɯos dn ɥsᴉuᴉɟ ɹǝɥ ǝpɐW

> —Anonymous (p. 51)

Here the meaningfulness and humor of the last line is lost unless the audience can actually see the printed poem. With poems such as this one, it is probably best to read them to small audiences that are close enough to see and appreciate the added meaning communicated by the form of the text as well as its content.

PREPARATION

Care must be taken to avoid the unique problems that poetry presents to the performer. Because of its musical quality, there is the tendency to read poetry with a sing-song intonation or to pause at the end of phrases, punctuation marks, or the end of each line. Think, for example, of how inappropriate it is to read Thayer's and Polacco's (1988) "Casey at the Bat" in this fashion (slashes indicate a pause):

> The outlook wasn't brilliant/
>   for the Mudville nine that day;/
> The score stood four to two,/
>   with one inning more to play./
> And then when Cooney died at first,/
>   and Barrows did the same,/
> A pall-like silence fell/
>   upon the patrons of the game./
>
> A straggling few got up to go/
>   in deep despair./ The rest/
> Clung to that hope which springs eternal/
>   in the human breast;/
> They thought, "If only Casey/
>   could but get a whack at that-/
> We'd put up even money now,/
>   with Casey at the bat."/

The solution here is to segment a poem into complete thought units and read each unit intact, thus placing pauses in between the thought units rather than at the end of each line. This alteration will create a more natural rhythmic and intonational interpretation that will, in turn, enhance the meaningfulness and appreciation of the poem by your audience.

> The outlook wasn't brilliant
>   for the Mudville nine that day;/

The score stood four to two,
  with one inning more to play./
And then when Cooney died at first,
  and Barrows did the same,
A pall-like silence fell upon
  the patrons of the game./

A straggling few got up to go
  in deep despair./ The rest
Clung to that hope which springs eternal
  in the human breast;/
They thought, "If only Casey
  could but get a whack at that-/
We'd put up even money now,
  with Casey at the bat."/

  A second problem to be avoided is misinterpretation created as a result of the relatively obscure nature of a poem. Consider the following poem by Grimes (1978):

My summer vacation …
went to Jones Beach with Jo Jo's family.
Jimmy got out of jail.
I sneaked into the pool crosstown twice.
Daddy lost his second job.
Mama said don't worry,
but he did.
Sharon's sister hit the number.
That makes the fourth time.
Teacher don't want to hear that.
What can I write?
Went to Jones Beach …

If performers aren't careful, they will read the first and last lines in this poem with a declarative intonational pattern, dropping the tone from medium on the word My to low on *vacation* in the first line and from medium on *Went* to low on *Beach* in the last line. This interpretation neglects the ellipsis that completes each line and undermines the intended sense that the child writer is pondering what to write, full well knowing that her teacher doesn't want to read about the experiences the girl really had during the summer vacation. These lines are better interpreted by reading the first word in the two lines with a medium tone then raising the tone up as you approach the last word in each line so as to raise a question in the listener's mind about the dilemma the young girl finds herself in.

Because poetry is compact in form, it naturally reads at a much faster pace than prose. This fact creates real problems for performers especially when reading a single narrative poem that is in picture book format. Because the text moves so quickly, the reader may not have sufficient time to adequately expose an audience to the accompanying illustrations. Such is the case with *The Sun's Asleep Behind the Hill* (Ginsburg, 1982), where several illustrations are purposely quite dark; *Playing Right Field* (Welch, 1995), where some elements of the illustrations are quite small despite the large format of the book; or *George Washington's Cows* (Small, 1994), where much of the humor is created in the fine detail of the illustrations. The easy solution to this problem would be to avoid reading these books to large groups of children as was suggested in chapter 2. But another possibility is to slow the pace of your reading way down and inject extended pauses frequently at the end of thought units all the while exposing the illustrations at sufficient length such that your audience can savor them.

In general, it is probably best to slow down the pace of reading poetry as compared with reading prose. However, there are times when speeding up the reading of a poem enhances its impact on an audience. This is often the case with those limericks which challenge the vocal nimbleness of the best performers, such as the following (The Peter Pauper Press, 1954):

> A canner, exceedingly canny,
> One morning remarked to his granny:
>   "A canner can can
>   Anything that he can
> But a canner can't can a can, can he?"
> —Anonymous (p. 13)

Because of its brevity and naturally quicker pace, reading poetry aloud obviously creates greater opportunities for a reader to get tongue tied than normally is the case with prose. As such, you will have to practice reading poetry aloud more so than with prose to smooth out the many rough places that are likely to occur in your poetry performance.

Beyond these special precautions, you can select and prepare to read poetry using the general guidelines for the reading aloud of prose found in chapters 2 and 3. Those guidelines apply as well to poetry in picture book or chapter book (anthology) format. Just keep in mind that practicing what you have planned is as important, if not more so, with poetry due to its unique format.

DELIVERY

Once you have prepared your poetry material carefully, the delivery can be handled in exactly the same way as with prose text. Follow the guidelines in chapters 2 and 3 that are relevant to those situations where you will be reading poetry aloud as well as prose.

EXTENDED PRACTICE ACTIVITIES

Developmental Activities

1. Consider your attitude toward poetry. If it tends to be negative, begin reading for yourself the types of poetry that young children seem to prefer. Seek out poets such as Arnold Adoff, Gwendolyn Brooks, Aileen Fisher, Paul Fleischman, Nikki Grimes, Lee Bennett Hopkins, Langston Hughes, Myra Cohn Livingston, David McCord, Eve Merriam, Jack Prelutsky, Shel Silverstein, or Kay Starbird. Check with your local library for anthologies of poetry by these people or refer to the poetry chapters of major children's literature texts such as Huck's or Norton's for suggestions as to what poetry you might find enjoyable.

2. Using any anthology of children's poems and the research-based guidelines provided earlier, determine which poems children would find enjoyable and which they would tend to reject. A good place to begin would be with Ferris' (1957) *Poems Old and New*.

3. Using Silverstein's (1996) *Falling Up* or (1974) *Where the Sidewalk Ends*, decide which poems can't be read aloud without showing the accompanying illustration.

4. Using any poem, segment it off in thought units and then read it aloud pausing only at the end of those units. (A place to start would be to get hold of a copy of Thayer's "Casey at the Bat" and continue the analysis started on Pages 71–72.)

5. Using a poem in picture book format, decide where natural breaks in the text enable you to pause so that the illustrations can be displayed for some extended length of time (try using texts by Ginsburg, 1982; Small, 1994; Welch, 1995).

6. Practice reading tongue twister limericks such as "A canner, exceedingly canny" (Peter Pauper Press, 1954, p. 13) presented earlier or the following from Dennis (1967). Read the poems with some speed while attempting to maintain clear articulation.

A fly and a flea in a flue
Were imprisoned, so what could they do?
    Said the fly, "Let us flee!"
    "Let us fly," said the flea.
So they flew through the flaw in the flue.
                    —Author Unknown

There was a young fellow named Fisher,
Who was fishing for fish in a fissure,
    When a cod with a grin
    Pulled the fisherman in ...
Now they're fishing the fissure for Fisher.
                    —Author Unknown

Culminating Activities

1. Thoroughly prepare a poem in picture book format for reading aloud and then perform it for an appropriate live audience.

2. Prepare to read aloud selections from a poetry anthology and then perform them for an appropriate live audience.

PART II

TRANSITION
TO STORYTELLING

5

Sharing Stories
Through the Use of Props

One benefit to the performer when reading aloud is that the text of the story is visible so that forgetting the story sequence is next to impossible. With storytelling, of course, no text is available, and remembering the story sequence is one of the major challenges faced by the performer. When making the transition from reading aloud to storytelling, it might be wise for you as a beginning performer to develop a repertoire of stories that employ some sort of prop that reminds you of the story sequence. In this way, you will begin to sense what it is like to share stories with an audience much as a storyteller does yet have the textual support available to someone who reads stories aloud.

Mastering the art of presenting wordless picture books, felt board stories, or stories that involve manipulating objects on an overhead projector may be a good transition for you away from reading aloud toward the pure art of storytelling. Of course, for some of you, learning to manipulate props in addition to learning a story may be an additional distraction that makes the transition more than less complicated. In this case, you will be best off skipping prop-related story performance and starting immediately to learn to tell stories.

Because of their reliance on visuals and simple construction, most prop-related stories, especially felt board and overhead projector stories, are primarily intended for young children. Then, too, most wordless picture books are geared toward younger audiences, although some like Goodall's (1987) *The Story of a Main Street*, Rohmann's (1994) *Time Flies*, or Ward's

(1973) *The Silver Pony* are fairly sophisticated and can be shared with older audiences. If the props are attractive and large enough to be readily seen and recognized by the audience, they serve as an additional attraction to the story and help to hold the attention of even the youngest children. An additional benefit of these stories is that, once told by the performer, members of the audience can manipulate the props and retell the stories themselves—a great value in classrooms where teachers consciously intend to develop each child's competence in story creation either through speaking or writing.

From the beginning performer's perspective, the value of the prop-related story is that the visuals serve as a reminder of the story sequence. However, not all prop-related stories serve this purpose. Puppets, string stories, origami stories, paper-cutting or tearing stories, and the like are probably not good choices for the beginning performer because the things being manipulated relate only indirectly to the plot sequence. In addition, the manipulatives require additional skill development prior to the telling plus additional concentration during the performance. Rather, stories where the manipulatives serve as reminders of events in the plot offer the beginning performer the best transitional experience between reading aloud and storytelling. As such, the discussion here is confined primarily to the use of wordless picture books, felt board stories, and overhead projector stories.

WORDLESS PICTURE BOOKS

Simply stated, wordless books are a unique breed of picture book that rely entirely (or nearly so) on the illustrations to carry the plot of the story. In the most extreme instance, there is no text at all except for the book title and an identification of the author/illustrator. Such is the case with Briggs' (1978) *The Snowman*, dePaola's (1978b) *Pancakes for Breakfast*, and Turkle's (1976) *Deep in the Forest*. There are, however, some books with limited amounts of text that would also be lumped into this category—for example, Van Allsburg's (1982) *Ben's Dream*, and *Just a Dream* (1990) and Wiesner's (1991) *Tuesday*.

Selection

In choosing which wordless books to admit to your repertoire, the place to begin is with those books where the illustrations present an obvious and simple sequence of events that can be readily translated into narrative text. Turkle's (1976) *Deep in the Forest*, dePaola's (1978b) *Pancakes for Breakfast*, Carle's (1971) *Do You Want to Be My Friend*, Martin and Gammell's (1989)

Will's Mammoth, or Ward's (1973) *The Silver Pony* are good examples. You might wait for a while to try your hand at books such as those by Chris Van Allsburg or David Weisner because the plots of their books tend to be more complex or obscure. Then, too, with any wordless book, you may decide not to provide any narrative as you show the illustrations, preferring to let the illustrator's artistry carry the story as was originally intended. In some specific instances, the impact of the illustrations may be more powerful if nothing is said during the exposure of the wordless pages. In my view, such is the case with Van Allsburg's (1990) *Just a Dream*. The wordless pages here are quite dramatic, and the text that follows each is sufficient to render each illustration meaningful. Thus, there is no need to create additional narrative for these pages.

As is the case with any picture book, deciding which wordless books to read during a specific performance will require your making judgments about the appropriateness of the content of the story and the quality of the illustrations given the nature of the audience and setting in which the stories are to be performed. Refer to guidelines provided in chapter 2 for direction here.

Preparation

The major task in preparing to "perform" a wordless picture book involves constructing the text to accompany the illustrations. There is one major trap to avoid during the construction. If the book involves true narrative, you will want to avoid creating text that is more expository than narrative. What you don't want to do is simply describe the detail of each illustration. Rather you want to create a story in true narrative form that coincides with the illustrations. Begin by creating names and personalities for each of the characters. Using the illustrations as reference, create a setting for the story, determine what the initiating event and/or major plot problem is, and identify the point in the story that serves as the climactic moment when all of the suspense created by the major plot problem is finally dissipated. (For further help with this type of narrative plot analysis, refer to chap. 7.) In crafting the text, keep to using the past tense in true storytelling fashion rather than present tense, which typifies expository writing. Add dialogue, where appropriate, for variety.

As an example of what not to do and what to do, consider Turkle's (1976) *Deep in the Forest*, a wordless variant of "The Goldilocks and the Three Bears" story. Example 5.1 represents a descriptive rendering of the text. As mere description of the illustrations, the text is lifeless.

Example 5.1

<u>What Not To Do</u>

<u>What is being shown</u>	<u>What is being said by the performer</u>
Title Page	Read the title and author. This is a mother bear and her three cubs.
Copyright Page	This cub sneaks off toward a cabin in the woods.
Pages 1 & 2	The bear cub enters the cabin. There are bowls of oatmeal on the table and the beds in the bedroom are made. No one seems to be at home.
Pages 3 & 4	The bear cub smells the oatmeal.
Pages 4 & 5	The cub tries the oatmeal in Papa's bowl. It's too hot. He tries Mama's oatmeal. It's too cold. Baby's oatmeal is just the right temperature so the cub eats all of it.
Pages 6 & 7	The cub jumps into a big chair and almost gets his head caught in the back of it. In another chair, he doesn't seem too comfortable. But the third chair is a small rocker, just his size. He plays on it until it breaks.
Pages 8 & 9	The bear cub goes into the bedroom.
Pages 10 & 11	He bounces on a big bed and rips open the feather pillow on another bed.
Pages 12 & 13	While the cub crawls under the covers on a small bed, a family enters the cabin. There is a man, a woman, and a young girl with long, curly hair. They see the broken rocking chair.

Pages 14 & 15	While the cub is in the small bed, the man and woman notice that someone has tried eating their oatmeal.
Pages 16 & 17	The little girl sees her broken oatmeal bowl and begins to cry. Her parents see that something has happened to the two big chairs.
Pages 18 & 19	The little girl cries when she sees that the rocking chair is broken. She follows her mother and father into the bedroom.
Pages 20 & 21	In the bedroom, the adults see that their beds have been messed up while the little girl tries to straighten the coverlet on her small bed.
Pages 22 & 23	She uncovers the bear cub and all three begin to chase him.
Pages 24 & 25	The cub escapes into the woods ...
Page 26	and finds the mother bear.

By contrast, Example 5.2 is an example of narration created to coincide with the illustrations in Turkle's book.

	Example 5.2
	What To Do
What is being shown	What is being said by the performer
Title Page	Read the title and author. Many years ago one late October morning, Mother Bear and her three cubs were searching through the forest for a perfect spot to hibernate for the winter ahead. She had her hands full this particular day, for the two older male cubs seemed more intent on scrap-

ping with one another than searching for a den while, Betina, the youngest female cub, seemed always to be wandering off in search of some curiosity.

Copyright Page

While Mother's attention was turned to the squabbling cubs, Betina crept toward something she'd not ever seen before. It was a cabin tucked away in the forest and home to a family—the Olsons. There was Father and Mother Olsen and their young daughter, Marta.

Pages 1 & 2

They had gone for a short walk while the oatmeal Mother Olsen had made for breakfast cooled a bit. But Betina knew none of this. All that she knew was that something in the cabin smelled awfully delicious, so she nosed her way past the front door. Nothing that she saw, the bowls of food on the table, the chairs, even the beds in the room beyond, was familiar to her.

Pages 3 & 4

And although she thought, for just a moment, that this might not be a place where she should be, her curiosity (and her empty stomach) got the best of her.

Pages 4 & 5

Betina bounded up onto the table and stuck her nose in Papa's bowl of oatmeal. "Yeow!" she screamed. The hot oatmeal had burned her nose. Carefully, she dipped her paw into the second bowl. It seemed a bit too hot too but the smallest bowl seemed just right so she ate up all the oatmeal. But the empty bowl fell from her paws to the floor with a crash.

Pages 6 & 7

That done, Betina wandered over to a tall chair. She climbed onto the seat but soon

	got her head stuck. With claws dug in, she managed to pull herself free. The other chairs were much more fun to play on.
Pages 8 & 9	In the next room, Betina found some other things that looked like fun to play on.
Pages 10 & 11	(Say nothing.)
Pages 12 & 13	When the Olsons returned from their walk, they found the front door of their cabin open. "Look at this mess," said father. "Someone's been here while we were out!"
Pages 14 & 15	Hidden under the covers, Betina didn't hear the Olsens ...
Pages 16 & 17	... especially Marta who cried when she found her bowl ...
Pages 18 & 19	... and her chair broken to bits.
Pages 20 & 21	The bedroom was a mess as well. Father just couldn't imagine who could have made such a mess until....
Pages 22 & 23	With a rush, Betina bolted from the bed. Mother grabbed a broom and swatted at her while Father tried to catch the cub.
Pages 24 & 25	Scared out of her wits, Betina flew out the open door and hid behind a nearby log.
Page 26	Bye and bye, Betina found her mother safe and secure in their own home for the winter.

Note that it isn't necessary to provide text for every action taking place in the illustrations. Now and then simply allude to the pictures, which can communicate the necessary detail of the moment.

Once you have created the text, read it through several times out loud. Gradually begin to practice showing the pictures while reciting the text and relying less and less on looking at your copy of the narrative. Don't be concerned if you change the words from the original. This will happen naturally and is of little consequence as long as the basic meaning of the story is retained. Come to rely more and more on the picture cues to remind you of the plot sequence. At some point you will be able to tell the story without looking at the text at all. During this phase of practicing, begin to make decisions about finger pointing, length of exposure of each illustration, pausing, vocal variation, and the like just as you would do for any picture book (see chap. 2, for reminders here). Do make a conscious effort to make greater eye contact with your audience; the more eye contact, the better. Practice doing so by imagining an audience seated before you.

If you feel the need to make notes on the decisions you have made, do so using the same form as was used for regular picture books (chap. 2, p. 38).

Delivery

At some point in your practicing, you will have developed a good flow to the story. It is time to try it out on a live audience. Then simply deliver the story as you have practiced it.

FELT BOARD STORIES

Felt board story performances involve telling a story while placing figures made from felt on a display board. Typically the figures will be the characters in the story plus elements of the setting such as trees, grass, huts, fences, and the like. Consider the story "The Turnip" for which there are several variants in print (Domanska, 1969; Milhous & Dalgliesh, 1990). In the version I tell, there are eight figures: a large white turnip with large green leaves, a large piece of green felt that serves as the ground that covers the turnip root and on which the story characters stand, a figure for the father, the mother, the daughter, the family dog, the family cat, and a tiny mouse. Before telling the story, I press the turnip to the left side of the display board and then cover its white root with the green ground piece, spreading it across the bottom of the display board and letting the leaves of the turnip flop down over the ground. As I tell the story and introduce each of the characters in succession from largest to smallest, I place the figure of the character on the display board in its proper position. See Example 5.3 for greater detail regarding the telling of this story.

Example 5.3

"The Turnip"

(Prior to telling, place the turnip on the
board with the root of the turnip covered
by the ground piece. Let the turnip leaves flop
down over the ground.)

One day, Farmer Fred planted a turnip seed.
The turnip grew and grew until it became a great,
big, enormous turnip.

"It's time to pick that turnip," said Fred one
morning. So he put on his ham-and-beans shirt,
his corduroy pants complete with galluses, and
his hob-nail boots. He went outside and grabbed
onto the turnip leaves. Then he began to pull
and pull. But the turnip wouldn't come out of
the ground and Fred knew he needed some help.
So he called to his wife, "Fe Fi Fo Fum. I pulled
the turnip but it wouldn't come."

Now, Fred's wife had just come into the
kitchen. She was about to cook up some
breakfast when she heard Fred calling to her.
She ran outside and, right away, she knew what
the problem was. So she grabbed onto her
husband's pants while he grabbed onto the
turnip leaf. And they pulled, and pulled, and
pulled. But the turnip wouldn't come out of the
ground and they knew they were going to need
some help. So they called to their daughter who
was over feeding the chickens: "Fe, Fi, Fo, Fum.
We pulled the turnip but it wouldn't come."

Well Fred's daughter came running over and could see, right away, what the problem was. So she latched onto her mother. Mother grabbed onto Fred, and Fred grabbed onto the turnip leaf. And, together, they pulled, and pulled, and pulled, and pulled. But the turnip wouldn't come out of the ground. And they knew they needed some help. So they called to the family dog who was sunning himself on the front porch: "Fe, Fi, Fo, Fum. We pulled the turnip but it wouldn't come."

Now the dog woke … and stretched (fore and aft) … and yawned, then meandered on over to the family. He could see, right away, what the problem was. So he latched onto the daughter. She latched onto her mother. Mom grabbed Pop. He grabbed the turnip leaf. And, together, they pulled, and pulled, and pulled, and pulled, and pulled but the turnip would not come up out of the ground. And they knew they were going to need some help. So they called to their family cat. The silly thing was over in the yard chasing its tail: "Fe, Fi, Fo, Fum. We pulled the turnip but it wouldn't come."

The cat stopped for a moment and thought: "I know what they want me to do. They want me to help them pull up that turnip. I don't like turnips, but then I haven't had much chance lately to bite the dog's tail." So the cat bit down on the dog's tail, the dog grabbed onto the daughter who latched onto her mother. She grabbed onto Fred and Fred grabbed the turnip leaf and the bunch of them pulled, and pulled, and pulled, and pulled, and pulled, and pulled. But the turnip wouldn't come up out of the ground and they knew they were going to need some help. The only problem was that there was no one left in the barn-yard to help. But the cat looked out into the field and saw a teeny, tiny mouse nibbling on an ear of corn. So they called to him: "Fe, Fi, Fo, Fum. We pulled the turnip but it wouldn't come."

Well, the mouse came scurrying in all
ready to help out. But the dog looked at him
and said: "You little thing, you. You can't help
us!" But the mouse squeaked: " I could pull that
turnip up all by myself. But since you've already
started, I'm going to let you help me." So the mouse
grabbed onto the cat. The cat latched onto the dog.
The dog grabbed the daughter. She grabbed onto
her mother who grabbed onto Fred. And Fred
grabbed the turnip leaf. And they pulled, and
pulled, and pulled, and pulled, and pulled, and
pulled, and pulled.

Then POP! Out of the ground popped the
turnip. And the little mouse turned on the dog
and squeaked: "See. I told you so."

And that's the story of the great big,
enormous turnip.

Felt Board Figure Construction

When constructing the felt board and figures, there are a number of considerations. You want to avoid purchasing small squares of felt that are stiff to
the touch. These pieces are permeated with sizing to make them stiff and
will not form a secure bond with the display board. Instead, go to a fabric
store and buy felt from the bolt. You can get this felt in a variety of colors and
in sufficient quantity to enable you to construct figures of almost any size.
Because this felt isn't sized, it will have a good nap and be flexible so that you
can press it firmly onto your display board. Try experimenting in constructing your figures. Use materials other than felt to add texture and dimension
to your figures (e.g., cotton balls for white hair, steel wool for a man's beard,
colored yarn for belts or suspenders, and various colors of felt or other material for clothing). When constructing a figure with multiple layers of material, I've found that it works best if you make a base for your figure entirely of
white felt. Then you can attach other materials over the base using a good
fabric glue; by having the base as one piece of felt, you will provide the figure
with the maximum amount of adhesion to your display board. You can add
detail and outlining by using a thin-pointed, permanent felt marker in some
dark color such as black.

For the display board, go to a lumber yard and ask for composition board (the kind of board that you can easily dig your fingernail into). You'll need a piece about 2½' x 3½', and you can often get a scrap piece this size for free or for a nominal fee at worst. Take a piece of 1" × 2" pine cut to a 3' length and, using large-headed nails, attach the pine to the back of the composition board about 4 inches from the top of the board and spaced evenly between the left and right edges (i.e., about 3" in from each side). Be sure that the large head of the nail is to the front side of the composition board and hammer the pointed ends of the protruding nails flat against the pine board. Attach two small eye screws to the ends of the pine board and connect them with a length of picture wire. This will serve as a convenient handle when transporting your board, which you will find easily portable because of its light weight. A large piece of felt can be used to cover the front side of the board to serve as the background and mounting surface of your felt board. However, I've found that a piece of burlap actually works better than felt because it has a more course nap than felt and, therefore, has more sticking power. Also burlap is cheaper than felt, but, if you use it, you might want to attach duct tape to the edges to prevent the burlap from unraveling. Whichever of the two materials you use, choose a neutral color (e.g., tan or white) to serve as a good background for your more colorful felt characters. Attach the covering on the backside of the board using a stapler. Stapling through the duct-taped edges will provide a more secure hold when using burlap.

At some time, you will find that both your felt figures and the felt or burlap backing lose their stickability (the color in the figures may also fade) and you'll need to replace both. It is wise, then, to keep extra material handy and a pattern of your favorite felt figures for ease in reproduction.

A variant of the felt board is the magnetic board where the display board is magnetic and the manipulated figures are backed by strips of magnetic material that adhere to the board. The beauty of this arrangement is that the figures typically adhere very securely to the board, thus preventing the figures from falling off the board at inappropriate times as will sometimes happen with felt characters, particularly if they have been used extensively. The disadvantage is that the display board is considerably heavier than a felt or burlap display board, and the materials needed to construct the figures are much more expensive than felt. The same is true for story boards and figures constructed from Velcro. In particular, the cost of sizable pieces of Velcro is prohibitive.

Selection

The best stories for translation into the felt board medium are those with relatively few characters and simple plot lines involving an obvious sequential pattern. This is so because, as is typically the case, only one performer is telling the story so that manipulation of the felt characters becomes a logistical concern. The simpler the story, then, the easier it is for one performer to handle the felt figures efficiently. It also helps if the settings are relatively simplistic so as to avoid the need to do too much scene changing with the felt figures. In fact, if the entire story can be delivered in one simple scene, you can mount the background scenery before beginning the telling and not have to worry about manipulating scene figures during the performance.

Preparation

There are basically two types of felt board stories: ones like "The Turnip," where you add felt figures to the display board as you progress through the story, or ones like *The Surprise* (Shannon, 1983), where all (or most) of the felt figures are on the display board prior to the story and the performer takes pieces off the board as the story is told. Each type of story has certain advantages and disadvantages. With the first type, there is always the worry that, in the heat of the performance, you won't be able to secure a figure to the display board and it will fall off, thus interfering with the flow of the story. In the second type, you can be certain to secure all the pieces before the performance but you have to take care when removing them during the performance (especially with figures that overlap one another) so that you don't expose a covered figure prematurely. With the latter type of story, you need to try out different ways of removing the pieces to determine which way works best. When telling *The Surprise*, which involves the uncovering of smaller and smaller felt figures of various shaped boxes placed one on top of another, I find that a pealing strategy enables me to take away the top figure while reaching underneath it to secure the next figure to the display board. I use a different strategy when removing the skirt, shall, witch hat, hair, and mask from the figure that represents the main character in Balian's (1994b) *Humbug Witch*. Because the figures partially overlap one another, I remove each figure in order sliding the skirt and shall downward, and the hat, hair and mask upward before removing them. In this way, the next level of figures remains in place until I want to remove it.

Timing the removal or placement of a figure on the display board is critical and must be kept simultaneous with the relevant text that you are speaking. Moreover, you want to manipulate the figures quickly so as not to interfere with the flow of the story. This requires extra concentration and, thus, a fair amount of practice to coordinate your telling and manipulating. Practice telling the story first while simply mimicking the placement of the figures on the display board. Once the flow of your telling is good, continue practicing, but add the actual placement of the figures on the display board.

Continue practicing while remembering to make as much eye contact with your audience as possible.

With the felt board story, as with picture book performances, limit the amount of gesturing, body movement, or facial expression to avoid competing with the felt characters, which should be the focus of the audience's attention.

When you have completed your preparation, you may want to make a record of your decisions by creating plot cards using the format introduced in chapter 7. Example 5.4 is a sample plot card outline of my version of Shannon's (1983) *The Surprise*.

Delivery

With sufficient practice to ensure the smooth and efficient telling and manipulation, you will have developed the confidence to perform your felt board story. An additional consideration in performing felt board stories involves the choice of some sort of support for the display board during the

---

Example 5.4

Plot Cards for a Felt Board Version of *The Surprise*

I. Bibliographic Information: *The Surprise* by George Shannon. Illustrated by Jose Aruego & Ariane Dewey. New York: Greenwillow, 1983. (Personal Collection)

II. Intended Audience & Rationale: Ages 2–5

Story Element	Developmental Trait
1. The young squirrel wants to please his mother and needs to be close to her.	1. Children this age require love & physical security from the family. Fear of separation from parents is considerable with young children.
2. Basic geometric shapes and common colors are introduced in the story.	2. Preschoolers are developing basic concepts including simple shapes and common colors.
3. The felt figures can be used by the children to retell the story.	3. Young children are physically very active; enjoy retelling stories and participating more actively/physically in stories.

4. The story is very simple and short.	4. Short, simple stories are consistent with the relatively short attention spans of preschoolers.

III. Personal Appeal:
  I love the simplicity of the tale and the fact that the main character, though young/small, is able to creatively solve his own problem.

IV. Average Time to Tell: 1 min. 35 sec.

V. General Notes:
  1. Place all of the felt pieces on the display board prior to the performance. Place squirrel under the cylinder box so that his nose is hidden but under the left edge of the box. Cover the cylindrical box with the triangle shaped box and, in turn, the circular, square then rectangular shaped boxes. Be sure each succeeding box completely covers the one before it. Place Mother squirrel to the left of the boxes and angled upward toward the top of the rectangle box.

  2. When removing the various box figures, peel them away from left to right while securing the figures underneath with your left hand if necessary.

  3. Position the felt board so that everyone in the audience can see it clearly & so that you don't block their view as you remove the figures.

Tailoring Notes
Anchor yourself
to the left of the
board to begin.
Pause/look at
audience before
beginning.

VI. Story Introductions:
  1. If your mother's birthday were two days from now, would you know what kind of a gift to get her? Discuss. Use the response of those in the audience who wouldn't know what gift to give and say: "Well, Squirrel had the same problem." Let's see if he's able to solve it.

2. Do you like surprises? Which do you like better—surprising someone or being surprised yourself? Either way, I think you'll find this story surprising.

Pause bet. Intro. & Story.

VII. Plot Analysis:

  A. Exposition: Who: Squirrel

           Where: No place specific

           When: Two days before some important holiday.

  B. Initiating Event (Plot Problem)

      Squirrel was worried
         (Had no gift for his mother)

  C. Rising Action:

    1. He'd searched through all the stores in town, but nothing seemed right.

    2. Mother had lots of clothes

    3. Squirrel had given her his drawings, stories, songs.

    4. He'd tried to make her cookies but burned them; a cake, but it flopped; a pecan pie? Forget it!

    5. "I'll just have to give her a plain old (holiday) card." But when he was about to put the stamp on, he had an idea.

    6. He called his Mother on the phone. "I'm sending you a package with a surprise inside. Open it right away!"

    7. The next day the package arrived. Mother took off the brown wrapping paper and found a red rectangular box with a

Point to figure of red box.

white and green ribbon. She opened it.	
8. Inside, there was a blue, square box with white top. She opened it.	Peel off red box
9. Inside, there was a yellow, round box with blue ribbon. She opened it.	Peel off blue box
10. Inside there was a green, triangular box with white trim. She opened it.	Peel off yellow box
11. Inside there was an orange, cylindrical box. She opened it.	Peel off green box; secure orange box to board.
D–F. Climactic Event (Plot Resolution) & Ending:	
And when she did, out jumped Squirrel. He leaped into his mother's arms and gave her a great big (holiday) kiss. (Squirrel gives Mother the gift of himself.)	Peel off orange box; move Squirrel next to Mother.
G. Follow-up:	
The story is in a book entitled "The Surprise" by George Shannon with illustrations by Jose Aruego & Ariane Dewey.	Show book

performance. An easel that has a ledge to support the board works well as long as the height of the board is sufficient for the seating arrangement of your audience. The sturdier the easel, the better particularly for stories that involve your placing the felt figures on the board during the performance. With an easel that provides sturdy backing, you can press the figures firmly onto the board and be more assured that the figures will stay in place. It is also important for the display board to be angled slightly backward for the same reason. Avoid hanging the display board perpendicular to the floor because it will be much more difficult to adhere your figures to the board.

A sturdy easel works best if you don't have to transport it from one place to another. If you plan to travel with your felt board stories, invest in a lightweight and collapsible stand that provides sufficient support for your display board. (I purchased an aluminum one that came with a magnetic board. Although I rarely use the magnetic board, I use the stand whenever I tell felt board stories.) Be certain that the stand has rubber (avoid plastic) skids on the bottom of the legs to prevent the stand from sliding on floors with smooth surfaces.

OVERHEAD PROJECTOR STORIES

Overhead projector stories are similar to felt board stories in that figures are manipulated as the story is being performed. Although the space you have to work on is much smaller for the projected story than with the felt board (limited to the size of the projector's glass surface, which is approximately an 8-inch square), the images created by the projected figures are typically much larger than the average felt figure. Thus, overhead projector stories are ideal for use with very large audiences, although they can be used with smaller audiences as well. Also, because of the nature of the overhead projector, the performer is able to directly face the audience at all times—a small advantage over the felt board story where, for at least part of the performance, the teller must turn away from the audience to manipulate the felt figures.

Overhead projector stories offer basically the same benefits as do felt board stories, but one dramatic difference involves the color of the figures that are projected. Silhouette projections are dramatic in appearance due to the high black–white contrast created by using opaque materials for the figures. But color projections can also be created via the use of colored acetate or felt markers intended for use with the overhead projector. These color projections will be brilliant and neonish in tone and, thus, very attractive to audiences. In addition, it is possible to do color combining to create secondary colors from primary ones. This capability enables the performer to tell stories that employ color combining such as Lionni's (1959) *Little Blue and Little Yellow*, Tison and Taylor's (1971) *The Adventures of the Three Colors*, or Jonas' (1989) *Color Dance*. Regardless of whether the projections are black silhouette or colored figures, the visual effect is unique and striking.

Figure and Background Construction

For any overhead projector story, create your background scenes by using sheets of clear acetate. Using felt markers made especially for use on the overhead projector, draw each scene on a single sheet of acetate. The simplest scenes are drawn in black, but consider using various colored inks for a more dramatic effect. Permanent scenery images can be made by drawing the scene on 8½" x 11" paper and then transferring the image onto a transparency via a photocopier.

The construction of the figures will depend on the type of projected story you want to create. As a general rule, you want to keep the number of figures you have to manipulate during an entire performance to a minimum; the simpler the operation, the better. For silhouette stories, sometimes referred to as *shadow stories*, any opaque paper material will work but, because it is easiest to manipulate stiff figures, oak tag is a good choice. Use a pair of scissors to cut out the figure in outline form and then add detail internal to the figure using a sharp pointed craft knife with a razor edge. The sample figures shown here (see Fig. 5.1) are taken from Joy's (1981) *Shadow Characters for Storytelling*. The first four figures are of the troll and the three Billy goats from "The Three Billy Goats Gruff." The fifth is a witch that can be used in a number of stories and is hinged so that it is possible to add movement to the figure. Joy explains that the hinge is made from a one-inch piece of thin wire bent and attached to the two halves of the figure as follows (see Fig. 5.2). Two strips of clear, stiff acetate are taped to each half as shown in the diagram so that performers can manipulate the figure without their hands appearing on the projection screen.

A second type of overhead projector story involves figures of various colors rather than silhouettes. Construction of these figures can be completed in two ways. The first involves using varied colors of transparent acetate for the full figure with outlines or detail created using dark-colored felt markers or by crafting oak tag frames (which will appear as a black outline on the projection screen) and then taping pieces of colored acetate to the frame. The second way involves using clear acetate for the full figure with detail and coloration provided by using various colors of felt marker. In either case, the figure can be either monotone or multicolored.

When creating your figures, take care to experiment with the various types of art materials available to you. With felt markers, for example, sometimes the color that is actually projected on the screen is not the same as the color indicated on the marker. Also, some colors will evaporate from your acetate because of the heat generated from the overhead projector. You need to find markers that are made specifically for use with the overhead. Check with an art supply store for markers such as Prismacolor.

Also know that when coloring with the felt markers, the figure will have a splotchy appearance, whereas a clear appearance is created with the use of colored acetate. Relatively inexpensive packets of 8½" x 11" sheets of red,

Figure 5.1

Troll

Little Billy Goat Gruff

Middle Billy Goat Gruff

Big Billy Goat Gruff

Witch (with movable parts)

Figure 5.2

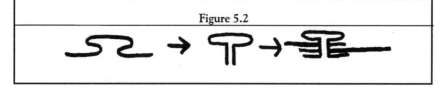

---

blue, yellow, green, and clear acetate can be purchased at art or office supply stores. The primary colors can be combined to create orange, purple, and gray, and all colors created by using colored acetate are true. Avoid attempting to create multicolored figures by using various colored sheets of a heat-resistant transparent film such as Zip-a-Tone. I have experimented with these films and they simply don't work because the film, no matter what the color or tone, is too dark and creates a gray shadow figure when projected rather than the colored figure that you would expect to get.

If the story you have chosen to re-create is in picture book form and is intended for children in an educational setting, it may be to their advantage that you craft your figures using the book illustrations as your models rather than creating wholly new figures. This will enable your audience to make an immediate association between the figures and the book, thus serving as an enticement for the children to read the book. One caution here. You must seek permission from a book publisher and/or illustrator for illustration reproduction if you intend to tell your shadow stories for profit, and their use cannot be covered by the fair use clause of the copyright law, which covers reproduction for educational purposes only. If you have any doubts as to whether your situation qualifies as fair use, it is best to check with the publisher beforehand.

When crafting figures for use on the overhead, you'll need some basic equipment. A thin piece of wood cut in a 1-foot square will serve as a good cutting board and protection for the desk or table where you do your work. A sharp-pointed craft knife with a razor edge is a must especially for cutting out intricate designs (avoid using other kinds of razor blade knives for this purpose). A pair of scissors, a pencil for drawing or tracing, and sheets of paper, oak tag, or colored acetate are needed. I have found that a goose-necked lamp that enables you to lower it right over top of your work helps in drawing and cutting intricate details. I like to keep an 8" × 8" square of oak tag handy as a template for the glass surface of an overhead projector. In that way, I can determine in a rough way whether the size of the figures and their arrangement on the projector will work. Although it is easier to cut figures from paper (especially if there is much intricate detail), I'd recommend that you use oak tag instead because oak tag is much more substantial, less likely to tear apart, and, because of its relative stiffness, easier to manipulate during a performance. If you plan to have children handle the figures, you would be wise to laminate your figures once they have been cut out. Because your figures will wear out in time, save some time in the long run by initially making a spare set of figures in laminated oak tag to serve as a template for later figure reproduction.

Selection

Although simply constructed stories are a good bet for use with the overhead projector, the medium allows for more complexity in setting and characterization than with felt board stories. Scene switching, even for one performer, is relatively easy if each different scene is on a single sheet of acetate. As seen earlier, greater variation in character is possible here because, with shadow figures at least, you can employ dramatic movement. In addition, specific types of stories seem to lend themselves well for use with the overhead projector because of the unique attributes of this medium. In a project devoted to shadow puppetry, an art form closely related to shadow overhead projector stories, a graduate student of mine noted that ideal stories include fantasy in general and tales involving magic, transformations, flight, sudden appearances and disappearances, cumulative tales, and "eating stories," where the main character eats and sometimes disgorges strange things (Ross-Albers, 1989, p. 9). Good choices, then, would be such stories as *The Fisherman and His Wife* (Zemach & Zemach, 1966) or *The Stonecutter* (McDermott, 1975), which involve magic and transformation; *Sun Flight* (McDermott, 1980) and "The People Could Fly" (Hamilton, 1985), involving flying; *Once a Mouse* ... (Brown, 1961), with its multiple appearances and disappearances, *The Napping House* (Wood & Wood, 1984) and *It Could Always Be Worse* (Zemach & Zemach, 1976), which are cumulative in format; and "eating stories" like *Gregory The Terrible Eater* (Sharmat, 1980) or *There Was An Old Lady Who Swallowed A Fly* (Taback, 1998).

Preparation

As with felt board stories, preparation for overhead projector stories involves learning to tell the story and learning to manipulate the figures in conjunction with the telling. Employ the same sequence in accomplishing these tasks as you did for felt board stories, developing the telling first and then practicing the telling and figure manipulation in tandem until the entire process is fluid. Basic manipulation of the overhead figures in a simple story is much easier than with felt board figures because the overhead figures can be placed on the projector without your having to twist, turn, or stoop to do so, as you have to do with felt figures. Eye contact with your audience is always an important consideration so the goal in practice is to develop a co-ordinated flow between the telling and the figure manipulation, which enables you to maximize eye contact with your audience.

With the figures laid out next to the projector in the sequence you will use them, simply practice moving the figures smoothly on and off of the projector. With more complex stories, the trick is to carefully organize your manipulatives off to the side of the projector before using them and then think through what you will do with the figures once they have been displayed. This is critical particularly if some of the figures will be used several times throughout the performance and is the reason that practicing is so essential. No doubt you will experience some awkwardness with a more complex set of figures when you first start practicing, but continued practice will enable you to work out the logistical bugs through experimentation with various strategies for handling the figures.

While you are planning the performance, don't fail to overlook some special advantages of the overhead medium. Think, for example, of various ways to use the light or move figures in and out of focus for dramatic effect (to create a storm scene or for a magical transformation). Also note that figures can be partially exposed by placing them on an edge of the glass surface.

As before, when you have completed your preparation, you may want to make a record of your decisions by creating plot cards using the format introduced in chapter 7. Example 5.5 is a version of "The Stonecutter." Two recent publications of the story are by McDermott (1975) and Newton (1990). In comparing the two versions, Newton's, although a longer text, is more simply constructed with a more predictable ending (the Stonecutter finds happiness) that would be better suited for younger children. McDermott's text, by contrast, is more obscure in keeping with the Japanese folk tradition from which it comes. The ending, in particular, leaves open the question of the Stonecutter's fate. As such, it can be used with audiences of older children through adults. In Example 5.5, provision is made for using the story with either young or old audiences.

Delivery

Overhead projector stories require a darkened room during the performance, which will require you to prepare the room for this contingency immediately prior to the performance. You may need to enlist the aid of someone from the audience to pull window shades and turn off lights. Also think about the placement of the projector and projection screen relative to

Example 5.5

Plot Cards for an Overhead Projector Version
of *The Stonecutter*

I. Bibliographic Information:

For younger audiences:

The Stonecutter by Pam Newton. New York: G. P.
Putnam's Sons, 1990. (Northville Public Library)

For older audiences:

The Stonecutter: A Japanese Folk Tale. by Gerald
McDermott. New York: The Viking Press. 1975.
(Personal Collection)

II. Intended Audience & Rationale:

Story Element	Developmental Trait
[For Young Children, Ages 3–5 (happy ending version)]	
The stonecutter finds happiness in being himself.	Children this age like stories that offer reassurance, esp. regarding sense of self; require happy endings.
[For Older children–adults (obscure ending)]	
The Stonecutter's fate is uncertain by story's end.	These people can handle obscure and less than happy endings.

III. Personal Appeal:

I love the simplicity of the tale (which makes it a good choice for
the overhead projector) and the universality of the major theme,
which involves valuing one's own talents and uniquenesses—a
message of value for all ages.

IV. Average Time to Tell: 1 min. 35 sec.

V. General Notes:

  1. Listing of figures:

      -Mountain part

      -Whole mountain

      -Stonecutter working

      -Stonecutter standing

      -Spirit

      -Prince

      -Procession scene

      -Sun

      -Storm Cloud

      -Another stonecutter

  2. Prior to performance, place mtn. part on right edge of overhead, working stonecutter on border mtn. Cover stonecutter with whole mtn. Turn off light.

  3. Position the overhead or audience so that everyone can see clearly & so that you don't block their view as you work the figures.

  4. When removing figures that appear only once, put them to the right of the projector.

  5. Place other figures in order of appearance in front of you (therefore, position overhead in the middle of a desk)

<u>Tailoring Notes</u>
Anchor yourself to
The left of the
projector.
Pause/look at
audience before
beginning.

VI. Story Introductions:

  1. If audience is familiar with a stone structure, ask if they know how the stone got there; if they think being a stonecutter would be an easy or difficult job; whether or not they or anyone would like that kind of a job. Keep these thoughts in mind as I tell you the story of "The Stonecutter."

2. You may have heard the saying: "The grass is always greener on another's side of the hill." Discuss its meaning and whether or not folks believe the adage applies to them. Though this story doesn't involve grass it does involve grassy mountains where, presumably, someone could believe in the adage.

VII. Plot Analysis:
    A. Exposition: Who: Stonecutter
        Where: Mountains of
            central Japan
        When: Many years ago.
	Pause bet. Intro. & Story. Turn on light to begin. Take whole mtn. off Stonecutter when introduced. Put whole mtn. after cloud on table in front of you. Put Spirit next to mtn. part when introduced

B. Initiating Event (Plot Problem):
        Stonecutter sees Prince
        (Stonecutter is unhappy with
           his lowly status)
	Remove mtn. Part (put to right of projector), Spirit (put on right edge of proj. out of sight). Put standing S'cutter in lower left corner, procession scene in middle with Prince on litter.

C. Rising Action:
        1. S'cutter wishes to be Prince.
           Spirit grants wish.
	Remove procession. Show Spirit. Put S'cutter over Prince.

2. S'cutter happy; tends garden
           &notes sun's power to wilt
           flowers. Wishes to be sun.
           Spirit grants wish.
	Put sun on top of display. Remove Prince. Bring S'cutter from out of focus & put on sun.

3. S'cutter happy; burns land.
           Cloud covers sun. S'cutter
           notes cloud's power; wishes
           to be cloud. Spirit grants
           wish.
	Hold cloud out of focus, remove sun & S'cutter. Move cloud into focus & put S'cutter in it.

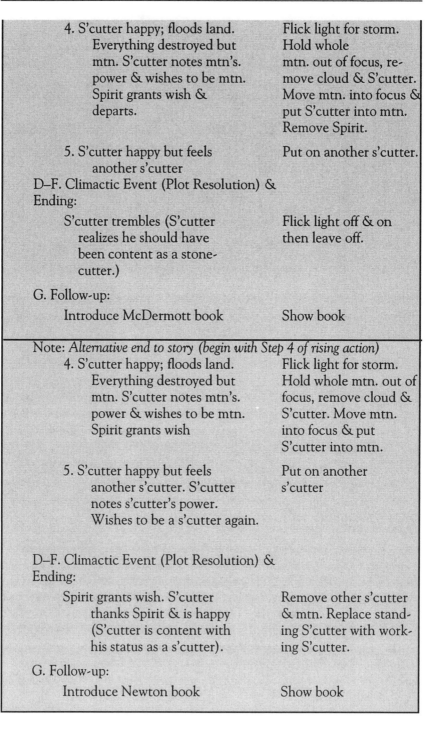

4. S'cutter happy; floods land. Everything destroyed but mtn. S'cutter notes mtn's. power & wishes to be mtn. Spirit grants wish & departs.

Flick light for storm. Hold whole mtn. out of focus, remove cloud & S'cutter. Move mtn. into focus & put S'cutter into mtn. Remove Spirit.

5. S'cutter happy but feels another s'cutter

Put on another s'cutter.

D–F. Climactic Event (Plot Resolution) & Ending:

S'cutter trembles (S'cutter realizes he should have been content as a stonecutter.)

Flick light off & on then leave off.

G. Follow-up:

Introduce McDermott book

Show book

Note: *Alternative end to story (begin with Step 4 of rising action)*

4. S'cutter happy; floods land. Everything destroyed but mtn. S'cutter notes mtn's. power & wishes to be mtn. Spirit grants wish

Flick light for storm. Hold whole mtn. out of focus, remove cloud & S'cutter. Move mtn. into focus & put S'cutter into mtn.

5. S'cutter happy but feels another s'cutter. S'cutter notes s'cutter's power. Wishes to be a s'cutter again.

Put on another s'cutter

D–F. Climactic Event (Plot Resolution) & Ending:

Spirit grants wish. S'cutter thanks Spirit & is happy (S'cutter is content with his status as a s'cutter).

Remove other s'cutter & mtn. Replace standing S'cutter with working S'cutter.

G. Follow-up:

Introduce Newton book

Show book

your audience and to the side of the projector from which you will be operating. If you are right handed, you will probably work best by standing to the left of the projector as you face the audience. To avoid blocking an audience member's view to the screen, either move the projector and screen or the audience so that the projector and screen are to the left of your audience as you face them. For a left-handed performer, simply reverse the directions in these instructions. Once these practical matters are cared for, simply deliver your story as you have practiced it.

UNIQUE PROP STORIES

One good transition story involving the use of props other than those mentioned earlier is Fleming's (1992) *Lunch*. In this story, a hungry mouse eats his way through a variety of vegetables and fruits. Before the performance, fill a large grocery bag with the actual foods (or pieces of food like a slice of watermelon wrapped in clear plastic wrap) mentioned in the story and then pull one food after another from the bag as you tell the tale. The children can actually help you tell this story if, when pulling the foods from the bag, you expose only a small part of the vegetable or fruit. The children will automatically guess the name of the food.

Other types of stories that employ unique props include string stories, paper-cutting stories, or stories that involve drawing a picture or manipulating a puppet or some other artifact such as a candle. Although these types of stories are fascinating, they tend not to be the best type of transition stories because the props used don't readily serve as reminders of the plot sequence. However, if you are interested in these types of stories, consult Pellowski's (1984) *The Story Vine*, Philpot's (1994a) *Scissor-Tales for Any Day: Storytelling Cutups, Activities & Extensions* and (1994b) *Scissor-Tales for Special Days: Storytelling Cutups, Activities & Extensions*, Druce's (1993) *Chalk Talk Stories*, Marsh's (1994) *Paper Cutting Stories for Holidays & Special Events* and (1992) *Paper Cutting Stories from A to Z*, and Painter's (1990) *Storyhours with Puppets and Other Props*. Other relevant texts are provided in the Resources listing at the end of this chapter.

EXTENDED PRACTICE ACTIVITIES

Developmental Activities

1. Visit your public library and find their collection of wordless books. Review some of these books and determine which could be readily translated into narrative text; that is, which would contain an obvious and simple sequence of events.

2. Choose one wordless book and develop a simple plot outline for it. Identify the setting and create names for the characters. Follow other guidelines provided in this chapter.

3. Locate fabric stores that sell felt by the bolt, burlap, and fabric glue. Obtain a suitable piece of composition board from a lumber yard and construct a felt board following the directions in this chapter.

4. Choose a favorite story and create felt characters for it following the guidelines in this chapter.

5. Locate art and/or office supply stores that carry packets of colored acetate, sheets of oak tag, craft knives, and felt markers for overhead projectors.

6. Keeping an overhead projector handy, experiment with your materials. Test the projected colors of all your felt markers and make notes on the nominal color and actual projected color of each. Try color combining multiple sheets of colored acetate and make notes on the various combinations. Try your hand at cutting shadow figures from sheets of oak tag using a craft knife. With a figure, try bringing it into and out of focus by lowering and raising the figure from the projector's light source to its glass surface. Try orienting the figure in different positions on the glass surface for special effect. Practice flicking the projector light off and on in rapid succession.

7. Choose a story appropriate for conversion to an overhead projector performance. Decide which figures need to be created to effectively perform the story. Keep the number of figures to a minimum and construct each figure so that it can be used multiple times, if necessary, during the performance. The fewer the figures you have to manipulate, the better. Follow the guidelines provided in this chapter.

Culminating Activities

1. Thoroughly prepare a wordless picture book for performance and then share it with an appropriate live audience.

2. Using the felt characters you've created, thoroughly prepare a felt board story and then perform it for an appropriate live audience.

3. Using the figures you've created, thoroughly prepare and overhead projector story and then perform it for an appropriate live audience.

RESOURCES

Anderson, P. (1963). *Storytelling with the flannelboard*. Minneapolis, MN: T.S. Denison.

Bay, J. (1995). *A treasury of flannelboard stories*. Fort Atkinson, WI: Highsmith.

Briggs, D. (1992). *Flannel board fun: A collection of stories, songs, and poems*. Lanham, MD: Scarecrow.

Chadwick, R. (1997). *Felt board story times*. Fort Atkinson, WI: Highsmith.

Hicks, D. (1996). *Flannelboard classic tales*. Chicago: American Library Association.

Joy, F. (1992). *Whole language for the holidays*. Torrance, CA: Good Apple.

Krepelin, E., & Smith, B. (1994). *Ready-to-use flannel board stories, figures & activities for ESL children*. Oakland, CA: Center for Applied Research.

Sierra, J. (1996). *Multicultural folktales for the feltboard and readers' theater*. Phoenix, AZ: Oryx.

PART III

STORYTELLING

6

Introduction
to Storytelling

Storytelling is a communication art that has existed since the dawn of civilization. Beyond this general notion, formal definitions of *storytelling* are hard to come by. Indeed, there has been some resistance within the current storytelling community to define the term. Open discussion of the topic was lively and adversarial during the 1997 National Storytelling Conference in Indianapolis.

Although there have been few attempts to define storytelling formally, its tenure throughout human history suggests that it is both a unique and valued commodity—one that is not likely to disappear from the scene regardless of whether a definition exists. But the lack of a clear definition makes talking about storytelling difficult and can create confusion for the beginning storyteller. Is taking photographs with Kodak ("America's Storyteller") equipment and film storytelling? Can professionals who appear at storytelling festivals and sing, dance, play musical instruments, juggle, or manipulate puppets be said to be storytelling? Are professional educators storytelling when, in a "storytelling" workshop, they read aloud from a text? Are the claims of researchers whose studies involve the significance of storytelling likely to be misleading when it is clear that reading aloud or the writing and dramatizing of stories rather than storytelling is the operative mode of delivery (Campbell & Campbell, 1976; Doss, 1982)? The existence of distinct terms such as *photographing, singing, dancing, reading aloud,* and the like implies that storytelling is somehow distinct from these other activities. What then is storytelling in its purest sense?

Roney (1998) has provided the following definition:

> In its most basic form, storytelling is a process whereby a person (the teller), using mental imagery, narrative structure, and vocalization or signing, communicates with other humans (the audience) who also use mental imagery and, in turn, communicate back to the teller primarily via body language and facial expressions, resulting in the co-creation of a story. (p. 23)

Accompanying the definition is a diagram (see Fig 6.1) of the process and a fuller exploration of the concept.

The arrows in the diagram exemplify both the artistic and communicative nature of storytelling. The language (vocalization and gesturing) used by the teller creates a reaction by the audience members who communicate their reaction back to the teller via body language, facial expression, and, sometimes, overt vocalization. In turn, these reactions influence the teller's continued language choices. The story, then, is a product of the continual co-creative interaction of both the teller and audience, who communicate with one another in cyclical fashion throughout the experience. As such, storytelling is an immediate and personal endeavor where each telling of a story is unique—a creation in this time and this place with this teller and this audience, never to be duplicated in precisely the same way again. The power and uniqueness of storytelling as a communication art rest in its co-creative, interactive, immediate, and personal nature and render it quite distinct from acting, singing, dancing, reading aloud, and related communication arts.

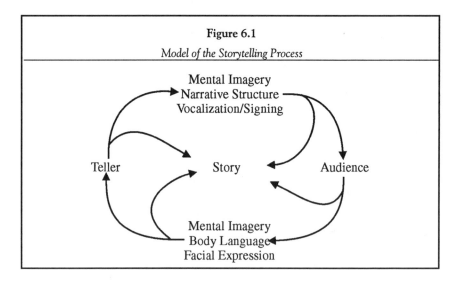

Figure 6.1

Model of the Storytelling Process

STORYTELLING AND READING ALOUD

Although storytelling and reading aloud are forms of communication art, they are quite distinct in nature. Storytelling is a more immediate and personal medium than reading aloud because there is no book present to intervene between the performer and the audience. The creativity is more flexible and instantaneous because the teller isn't locked into the book text as is the case with the reader. The communication between teller and audience is more direct, and the sense the audience members have is that they are more dramatically involved in the creation of the told story. Thus, the experience appears, from the perspective of the audience, to be more personal. As such, storytelling is a more powerful medium than reading aloud. It is not uncommon for observers to report that storytelling audiences appear mesmerized when listening to a storyteller.

THE PERSONAL NATURE OF STORYTELLING

For the beginning storyteller, the highly personal nature of storytelling is an attribute that may cause some concern. Unlike acting, where the performers hide behind the personalities of the characters they play, storytellers represent themselves on stage. Audiences will know who you are by virtue of your choice of stories and mode in which you delivery them. Putting yourself before audiences, particularly ones with which your are not too familiar, and sharing with them your fundamental personality through your storytelling is risky business. In this situation, you may experience a natural fear of being personally rejected. To counter this anxiety, it is important for you to remember the co-creative and interactive nature of storytelling. Storytelling audiences are very supportive of the teller because the success of a storytelling relies on teller and audience working together. If the teller fails, so also does the audience. Naturally, then, audiences provide support and encouragement to the teller because they have a vested interest in the success of the telling, which they are co-creating along with the teller.

THE VALUE OF STORYTELLING

Storytelling is arguably the oldest form of literary communication and has served generations of humans as their major means of entertainment. But its longevity must be due as well to its value as a tool for edification. The collected narratives of a culture represent its history, values, knowledge, beliefs, and rituals. The traditional means of transmitting this collective wisdom from one generation to the next has been storytelling. Thus, storytelling enables humans to connect with their past and present culture through narrative. As such, it serves as the foundation for self-identity. However, storytelling also provides people with a window to other cultures. By hearing stories from traditions other than our own, we become more aware of the differences and similarities among people and develop a greater tolerance for others and a better sense of our own place in the world.

Moreover, narrative is the major means by which humans make sense of the world (Moffett, 1983, p. 49). As such, storytelling is the natural way for people to learn about their world. But stories, particularly communicated through storytelling, are emotion ladened and generate an affective as well as a cognitive response in an audience. Thus, the learning that takes place via storytelling impacts one's knowledge as well as one's attitude toward that knowledge and the learning process. Simply stated, storytelling is a natural and enjoyable way for humans to teach and learn.

Obviously, then, storytelling is a valuable commodity in the formal educational setting. For the youngest school-age children, using storytelling as a teaching and learning strategy is consistent with the way in which preschoolers learn to master spoken language. Roney (1993) noted the similarities between the process of language acquisition and the value of children involved in storytelling, primarily as members of an audience. The significant implication here is that storytelling is an excellent activity for children who are developing literacy skill because the process of engaging in storytelling closely mirrors the process of reading and writing as well as listening and speaking. As was the case with reading aloud, storytelling provides children with vital background knowledge that makes success in learning to read and write possible. Roney (1989) has provided detailed descriptions of three lesson plans incorporating storytelling into K to 12 classrooms.

To date, little research exists that involves the effect of storytelling on humans. Relative to research involving reading aloud, there are far fewer studies of the effect of storytelling on the cognitive and affective aspects of a child's growth toward literacy. Bailey's (1970) study resulted in significant gains in psycholinguistic capability of the first-grade children who were the subjects of this research. But storytelling was only one of several treatments, and the effects of the storytelling alone were not isolated from the total effect of the multiple treatments.

Amato, Emans, and Ziegler (1973) studied the effect of storytelling and creative dramatics activities on fourth- and fifth-grade pupils in a public library setting. The students in the storytelling treatment groups listened to two told stories and four recited poems during half-hour sessions offered, presumably, once a week for 28 weeks in each of two successive years. The results indicate that there was no significant difference in the pupils' interest in books or in reading achievement when comparing the pupils who listened to stories with pupils in a control group. However, some evidence suggests that the pupils' self-image's and creativity were significantly affected by the storytelling experience.

In a year-long study where kindergarten and first-grade children whose teachers told stories to them were compared to same-grade children whose teachers did not tell stories, it was discovered that the children in the experimental group grew significantly in their ability to create a new story, although no significant difference was found in their story retelling ability (Farrell & Nessel, 1982). Unfortunately, the researchers did not indicate in their report the amount of storytelling that actually took place in the experimental classrooms, so the practical application of this research is limited. Additional studies that make claims as to the effectiveness of storytelling on children's achievement are of limited value due to design flaws that undermine the validity of their results (Froyen, 1987; Peng, 1989; Young, 1988).

As the use of storytelling in the classroom gains in popularity, it is likely that more research will be conducted to determine its efficacy as a teaching and learning strategy. For the time being, however, it is important to recognize its lengthy tenure in human history as the premier medium of acculturation.

THE ART OF STORYTELLING

At the heart of the art of storytelling is its co-creative nature. This nature, along with the immediacy of a storytelling performance, sets storytelling apart as unique among all the arts. The story, which is the product of a performance, is not just the creation of the performer but of the performer and audience in concert with one another. In no other art form, then, is the relationship between performer and audience so dramatic or critical to the success of the artwork.

The primary responsibility for creating the art of storytelling, however, rests with the performer. As is the case with reading aloud, that responsibility is best exercised when the storyteller carefully and thoughtfully prepares for a performance. The quality of the artistry is dependent on the care the storyteller takes in selecting stories and preparing those stories for sharing with audiences.

7

Stand-up
Storytelling

The ultimate experience in sharing stories with an audience involves stand-up storytelling where the teller uses no props of any sort to deliver the story. Although selection is an important process no matter what the mode of delivery, it is unquestionably the most critical of the storytelling processes for a beginner.

SELECTION

In some ways, selecting literature to share with an audience via telling is no different than selecting literature to read aloud. The dualistic process remains the same—building your repertoire and then choosing stories for a specific performance. Similarly, you must truly enjoy the literature you choose to tell and must have a sincere interest in sharing it with an audience. Although the nature of your telling repertoire will be more limited than your read-aloud repertoire (that is, stories primarily), you will still want to vary the type of stories you tell based on the needs of your potential audiences. Teachers and librarians must continue to be conscious of the readability levels of the print versions of the stories they tell because many children will be motivated to read these versions following a performance. If the text includes any special elements (e.g., an unfamiliar dialect, a chant, or unusual sounds), which are essential to the nature of the story yet which you cannot master, it is better not to try to tell these stories.

When choosing stories from your repertoire for a specific storytelling performance, the criteria for selection remains the same as was the case with read-aloud texts. You can employ the Plot Concept, Theme–Trait Matching process just as you did when selecting literature to read aloud.

The Critical Task

For beginning tellers, there is one significant difference between choosing stories to tell as opposed to read aloud. Most beginners are much more apprehensive about telling stories to an audience (particularly an audience of peers) than reading aloud to them. From informal surveys of students in my graduate level storytelling class taken at the beginning of each term, I know this to be the case. Over the past two offerings of the course, for example, whereas 15 students suggested that they were anxious about reading aloud to peers, 22 indicated anxiety at the prospect of telling stories to peers. In addition, several students noted that the intensity of anxiety was much greater for storytelling than for reading aloud and much greater for performing for adults than for children.

Overcoming this apprehension, then, is the single most critical task facing the beginner, is the key to becoming a successful teller, and is of far greater significance when choosing stories to tell than when choosing stories to read aloud.

At the heart of the beginner's concern is the fear of forgetting some important words in the story and thereby appearing to others to be incompetent, foolish, and vulnerable—an embarrassing prospect at best. This fear is created, on the one hand, by the belief that the successful storyteller employs word-for-word memorization and recall of a story and, on the other hand, the suspicion that forgetting some words in a story is personally inevitable. The way out of the dilemma is to abandon the notion that effective storytelling requires word-for-word memorization and recall. But told stories don't just appear out of thin air; they do come from one's memory. The issue then is to determine what about a story should be committed to memory (if not specific words) and how to go about this memorization so that recall is facilitated. But this is as much a selection issue as it is a preparation issue.

It is important to be clear about the objective here. If the biggest hurdle to becoming a successful storyteller is overcoming your anxiety about performance, then all that you do prior to performance must be for the purpose of nurturing your confidence as a teller and avoiding those practices that create the fear in the first place. In truth, you will probably always be a bit nervous prior to a performance. This is to be expected because, as mentioned in chapter 6, telling stories to an audience involves revealing your essential personality to people most of whom you've never met before. There will always be the fear, in this situation, that some people will reject you personally because of your personality. However, part of this nervousness is a result of your desire to tell the very best story possible for your audience and, as such, is natural and beneficial. What is to be avoided is anxiety to the extent that you freeze in front of an audience and are unable to deliver the story to them for both their and your mutual benefit.

This confidence building must commence at the very beginning of the process of becoming a storyteller—with the initial selection of stories to build your repertoire. First you must choose stories that you believe are right for you. There are no step-by-step guidelines to be followed here, just a certain sensation that a particular story is one that you just have to tell to others.

Stories From Your Read-Aloud Repertoire

A good place to start might be with certain stories from your read-aloud repertoire—those that you've read aloud so many times that you hardly look at the text anymore when reading. It's a good bet that you can put the book away and simply tell these stories. You don't need to worry about recalling the text word for word (although you may, in fact, use most of the exact wording of the original text). Because you know the story so well, you will feel confident substituting words or phrases for the original text now and then. Try telling these stories in private and, if you feel confident with them, take them to an audience. With a minimum amount of work, you will have begun to build your storytelling repertoire.

"Two-Minute" Tales

For all beginning storytellers, regardless of whether you can count on a read-aloud repertoire as a starting point, it is critical that you choose stories to tell that build your confidence; ones that you can easily learn to tell. I call this type of story the *Two-Minute Tale*, not so much because it is a story that can be told in 2 minutes (it could take more or less time than that to tell), but because the notion of 2 minutes suggests, metaphorically, that the story is relatively short and simple and, therefore, easy for you to learn to tell. It is a story where the progression of the plot is so logical and obvious to you that there is no need to memorize the text word for word. Recall is facilitated, in this case, because you have already mentally internalized the basic structure and logic of the story. All that is left for you to do is practice telling the story out loud in your own words to the point where you can deliver it fluidly and with appropriate emotion.

What constitutes a 2-minute tale will probably vary from one person to the next because what may appear logical and obvious to one may not seem so to another. However, some stories are constructed so simply that it is likely they will have broad appeal to beginning storytellers. This is often the case with folk tales, particularly ones from Western European and African cultures. But more contemporary stories also meet the criteria for a 2-minute tale and should be considered for inclusion into the beginning storyteller's repertoire along with the more traditional tales. One such story is Shannon's (1983) *The Surprise*:

> Squirrel was worried. His mother's birthday was one day away, and he still hadn't found her a present. He had looked in all the stores in town, but nothing seemed just right. She had perfume and books and the most beautiful garden. He'd already given her drawings, and songs that he'd made up. And every time he made a cake, he burned it. He sighed and said. "I'll just have to send her a plain old birthday card." But as he was putting the stamp on, he had an idea. He called his mother on the telephone and said, "I'm sending you a package with a surprise inside. Be sure to open it right away." The next day when the package arrived, his mother took off the ribbons and opened the box. But there was only another box inside. So she opened that box, and found another box. And opened that box and found another box. And opened that box, and found another box. And when she opened that box … Squirrel jumped out and gave her a kiss!

This story is quite simple, requiring only a few minutes to tell, and involves a commonplace occurrence—that of finding the right gift to give someone you love as a birthday present. Note, too, the internal logic of the story. As Squirrel's mother opens one box after another, the boxes become smaller and smaller until the one remaining box is appropriately "squirrel-sized." Then, too, the ending is highly predictable yet surprising and humorous.

Learning the story is relatively easy because it is likely that the important things to remember are already tucked away in your memory: the frustration of finding just the right gift for someone who "has everything," the commonplace occurrence of sending birthday cards, the fact that the boxes are progressively smaller, and the simple and appropriate ending of giving loved ones a kiss for their birthday. What is not important to remember are specific words. The gifts that Squirrel has already given his mother can be replaced by ones the storyteller remembers having given to friends or relatives. The construction of the various boxes can be whatever the teller wishes and can change from one telling to the next. Even the nature of the characters can change (It could be Mouse or Rabbit or Turtle instead of Squirrel) so long as you remember to keep the box sizes appropriate for your chosen character. In your retelling of this tale, then, you can feel free to substitute your own elements for these unimportant ones. Simply retain the essential structure of the story.

Research Support

There is evidence that beginning storytellers find the 2-minute tales easier to learn than a more complex story and that they feel more confident when dealing with the simpler story. Roney (1986) conducted research that involved adult beginning storytellers enrolled in a graduate level storytelling course. These students were introduced to both a 2-minute tale and a more complex tale requiring significant word-for-word memorization. Both tales took slightly over a minute to tell with acceptable fluidity. Following the introduction, the students were then requested to recall both tales; half retold the tales into an audiotape recorder and half rewrote the tales onto blank sheets of paper. Subsequently, they were surveyed as to which of the two tales was, in their opinion, easiest to remember and which was easiest to retell or rewrite. A significant number of these students responded that the 2-minute tale was both easiest to remember and easiest to recall.

Additional analysis of the retellings of those students who told both stories into a tape recorder revealed that they paused less frequently and uttered fewer mazes (e.g., *Ah, Um, Er*) when retelling the 2-minute tale than when retelling the complex one. They were also better able to retain in their retellings the essential elements of the 2-minute tale as opposed to the complex tale and were more effective in delivering the 2-minute tale than the complex one.

Additional analysis of the responses of those students who rewrote both stories revealed that they were better able to retain in their rewriting the essential elements of the 2-minute tale as opposed to the complex one. It is important to note that the major dependent variable in the research was student responses to survey questions, which, involved their opinion as to which of the two stories was easier to remember and recall. How these students felt about the relative ease of remembering and recalling the 2-minute tale as opposed to the complex one is of vital interest here because it is their beliefs (as opposed to any more objective determination as to which of the two stories was easiest to remember and recall) that ultimately determine the confidence level with which they tell the tales. Clearly they felt more confident retelling the 2-minute tale, and, as mentioned before, building confidence is the major objective for beginning tellers. To the extent that the results of this study are generalizable beyond the students taking part in the research, it appears that 2-minute tales are a good type of story for beginners to choose to build their confidence as tellers. A short list of 2-minute tales is provided in the References section at the end of this chapter.

Stories Not to Tell

For the beginning teller, certain stories are best saved for means of presentation other than storytelling. "The Elephant's Child," one of Kipling's (1952) *Just So Stories*, is a good example. Here the language of the story is so rich and integral to the beauty and power of the tale that delivering it to an audience requires that each of Kipling's words be retained in the presentation. This forces the presenter to memorize and recite the text word for word rather than tell the story—not a recommended practice for beginning tellers. Any story that employs poetic or verse text, and therefore requires strict memorization, should also be avoided. Similarly, Sendak's (1963) classic *Where the Wild Things Are* or such recently published stories as Nones' (1989) *Wendell*, Cowen-Fletcher's (1993) *Mama Zooms*, or Hobbs and Kastner's (1997) *Beardance*, all of which utilize illustrations that are vital in communicating the fullest message of the author and illustrator, should not be told. Rather, these stories are best saved for reading aloud.

Sources for Beginning Tellers

As a storyteller, you must also be a story consumer, constantly searching for stories to incorporate into your repertoire. Stories for telling are found basically in two forms—print or oral media. To begin, you will probably rely heavily on books as your main source of stories to tell. However, there is some logic to the notion that your best source of tellable tales should be the oral medium that you are striving to master. A story that is heard rather than read has a special vibrancy and life that can't be duplicated in even the best written text—just the thing you may need to convince you that this story is one you must learn to tell. I am currently investigating whether hearing a story as opposed to reading one makes learning stories any easier for beginning tellers. However, you may be encouraged to continue learning to tell stories if you avail yourself of as many opportunities as possible to hear other tellers. Seek out storytelling support groups such as the National Storytelling Network (NSN) or your local story league, which sponsor many storytelling events throughout the country. NSN publishes a list of active storytellers plus regional storytelling events, organizations, periodicals, and production companies. Through its publication entitled *Storytelling Magazine*, NSN provides a calendar of upcoming storytelling events in all regions throughout North America. A partial list of storytelling support groups is located at the end of the chapter.

Selecting From One's Repertoire for a Specific Performance

The process of selecting stories to tell for a particular performance is essentially the same as is the process for selecting stories to read aloud. The needs, interests, and capabilities of the members of the audience are of primary importance. Told stories can be matched to specific audiences through the Plot Concept, Theme–Trait Matching Process introduced in chapters 2 and 3.

PREPARATION

Once you have chosen a story for telling (or the story has chosen you as its teller), the care you take in preparing for its telling will likely determine how successful the actual performance will be. The essential concern is that you develop confidence in your telling—confidence that is developed only with thorough preparation prior to delivery.

What to Memorize and What Not to Memorize

Because the stories you tell are the products of your mind, memory plays a critical role in successful telling. The trick for you as a beginner in developing self-confidence is to avoid overextending your ability to recall the story during a performance. Rather than attempting to memorize a story word for word, which can lead to overextension and the potential of forgetting (particularly in a pressure situation such as telling to peers), commit to memory only the most basic structural elements of the tale. In other words, develop a mental outline of the story and then let this outline serve as a guide for you as you tell the story by simply "letting it happen" in your own words. If the tale you have chosen is a 2-minute tale, the structural progression of the story will be so obviously logical to you that little conscious memorization, if any, will be required. Most narratives follow a simplistic pattern known as the *melodrama*, which takes the form shown in Fig. 7.1. Using this format, then, the first task in your preparation should be to abstract from the text of your story its basic elements in outline form. An example of this process is presented next. Suppose you have chosen to tell "The Three Billy Goats Gruff" and are using Galdone's (1973) text as your original source. The full text of Galdone's version of the story is divided into segments using the melodrama rubric provided in Fig. 7.1 (see Example 7.1). Subsequently, I have provided an outline of the basic structure of the story (see Example 7.2).

Figure 7.1

Narrative Structure

Exposition—The story begins and the setting and main character (at least) are introduced.

Initiating Event—Something happens to create tension: a crisis, a conflict, or, at least, an anomaly; often identified as the plot problem.

Rising Action—Additional events add to the suspense created initially by the plot problem.

Climactic Event—Something happens to resolve the plot problem and dispense all the tension.

Falling Action—Any "loose ends" created during the rising action are resolved; optional, obviously, and deleted if no loose ends were created previously in the story.

Ending—The story is concluded.

Example 7.1

The Three Billy Goats Gruff

I. Exposition:	Once upon a time there were three Billy Goats. They lived in a valley and the name of all three Billy Goats was "Gruff." There was very little grass in the valley and
II. Initiating Event:	the Billy Goats were hungry. They wanted to go up the hillside to a fine meadow full of grass and daisies where they could eat and eat and eat, and get fat. But on the way up there was a bridge over a rushing river. And under the bridge lived a Troll who was as mean as he was ugly.
III. Rising Action:	1. First the youngest Billy Goat Gruff decided to cross the bridge. "TRIP, TRAP, TRIP, TRAP!" went the bridge. "WHO'S THAT TRIPPING OVER MY BRIDGE?" roared the Troll. "Oh, it's only I, the tiniest Billy Goat Gruff," said the Billy Goat in his very small voice. "And I'm going to the meadow to make myself fat." "No you're not," said the Troll, "for I'm coming to gobble you up!" "Oh, please don't take me. .I'm too little, that I am," said the Billy Goat. "Wait till the second Billy Goat

Gruff comes. He's much bigger." "Well then be off with you," said the Troll.

2. A little later the second Billy Goat Gruff came to cross the bridge. "TRIP, TRAP! TRIP, TRAP! TRIP, TRAP!" went the bridge. "WHO'S THAT TRIPPING OVER MY BRIDGE?" roared the Troll. "Oh, it's only I, the second Billy Goat Gruff, and I'm going up to the meadow to make myself fat," said the Billy Goat. And his voice was not so small. "No you're not," said the Troll, "for I'm coming to gobble you up!" "Oh, please don't take me. Wait a little, till the third Billy Goat Gruff comes. He's much bigger." "Very well, be off with you," said the Troll.

3. Then up came the third Billy Goat Gruff. "TRIP, TRAP! TRIP, TRAP! TRIP, TRAP! TRIP, TRAP!" went the bridge. The third Billy Goat Gruff was so heavy that the bridge creaked and groaned under him. "WHO'S THAT TRAMPING OVER MY BRIDGE?" roared the Troll. "IT IS I, THE BIG BILLY GOAT GRUFF," said the Billy Goat. And his voice was as loud as the Troll's. "Now I'm coming to gobble you up!" roared the Troll. "Well, come along!" said the big Billy Goat Gruff. "See what you can do!"

IV. Climactic Event:	So up climbed that mean, ugly Troll, and the big Billy Goat Gruff butted him with his horns, and he trampled him with his hard hooves, and he tossed him over the bridge into the rushing river.
V. Falling Action:	Then the big Billy Goat Gruff went up the hillside to join his brothers. In the meadow the three Billy Goats Gruff got so fat that they could hardly walk home again. They are probably there yet.
VI. Ending	So snip, snap, snout, This tale's told out.

Example 7.2

Outline of the Three Billy Goats Gruff

I. Exposition:	When—Once upon a time Who—Three Billy Goats Gruff Where—A valley with little grass
II. Initiating Event:	Goats hungry; want to go to meadow but a troll prohibits their passage there.
III. Rising Action:	1. Youngest Billy Goat crosses bridge. Troll threatens to eat him. Goat persuades Troll to wait for second, bigger goat who would make a better meal. 2. Second Billy Goat crosses bridge. Troll threatens to eat him. Goat persuades Troll to wait for third, biggest goat who would make a better meal. 3. Biggest Billy Goat crosses bridge. Troll threatens to eat him.
IV. Climactic Event:	Biggest Billy Goat disposes of Troll.
V. Falling Action:	1. Three Billy Goats Gruff get fat. 2. Probably still live in meadow.
VI. Ending:	"So snip, snap, snout. This tale's told out."

With the outline completed, you now understand the basic structure of the story. Commit that outline to memory by simply reading it over several times while visualizing in your mind what you are reading. Then put the outline aside and recite it out loud. Repeat the verbalizing until you are confident that you know the story structure. If there are unique phrases or sentences that begin and end the story or a chant that is repeated throughout the text, you may want to memorize them word for word. An alternative would be to revise the story so that neither the chant nor any specific beginning or ending is necessary, thus eliminating the need for any word-for-word memorization.

Now begin to tell the story out loud. Do this in privacy so that you won't be distracted and can concentrate on bringing to life that mental outline of the story. Consciously concentrate on the outline as you tell the story. If you find yourself stumbling through the telling or running into dead ends on the initial attempts, don't worry. Every storyteller, even the best professional, experiences difficulty when first learning a story. Fluidity will come as you continue to practice the story out loud and, at some point, you'll find yourself telling the story from start to finish with few glitches in the flow of the story.

Text Analysis

Some stories may present the teller with unique problems, and you may want to plan to deal with them well in advance of the performance. Again, the intent here is to build confidence via thorough preparation. Many of the textual problems associated with reading aloud will also be of concern when telling a story. If a unique sound or dialect is required, you have to decide if you are comfortable and qualified in using it. If either is irrelevant to the story, simply choose not to use it. If it is an important part of the story, practice using it to the point of mastery or delete the story from your repertoire.

Dialogue adds variety to a narrative but also requires special attention. It can be dealt with effectively through vocal variation or body movement. Change the pitch, volume, or tone when switching between the utterances of various characters. Mentally imagine the location of the characters in a conversation and assume those varied positions as you deliver the dialogue. For example, you might imagine that one character is taller than the other and situated to the right (as you face the audience). As you deliver this character's lines you might turn your head to the left and look down toward the floor. When the other character begins to speak, look up toward the ceiling and to your right. Do remember to be consistent in your use of vocal variation and movement so as not to confuse your audience. Also, don't abandon eye contact with your audience for any extended period of time. Remember that you are telling a story not dramatizing it. Moreover, you won't feel comfortable using these techniques unless you have practiced them to the point where you can employ them confidently prior to your performance.

Once your practice tellings are fluid, you can now begin to feel the mood changes in the story and work to incorporate mood interpretation into your telling. It is likely that you will have accurately monitored the mood of the story through your initial plot analysis. But you may want to revisit the original text and focus specifically on this aspect. When you have a clear sense of the varied moods in the story, begin to inject these feelings into your practice tellings. Vocal variation in volume, pace, and tone accompanied by varied facial expression is the most effective way to communicate mood. Be careful not to overplay the mood unless you are attempting to be humorous through caricature.

Chants, repeated phrases, and poems or songs that are integral to the story must be memorized word for word. But these elements do add seasoning to your telling and may be worth the extra time it takes to memorize them verbatim.

Self-Analysis

Because sincerity is critical in establishing a trusting relationship between you and your audience, it is important to know who you are as a person and then be yourself when telling stories. Don't try to be someone or something other than yourself. Knowing who you are should influence your preparation to tell stories. As you practice, think consciously about your posture, the way you move, the quality of your voice, your personal appearance, and especially the need to make direct eye contact with your audience.

Stand tall (feet about hip-width apart) or sit erect as you deliver stories. Avoid slouching unless you have consciously injected this posture into your story for dramatic effect. Beyond the appearance value of these postures, they facilitate comfortable breathing and communicate a sense of confidence to your audience. Consciously employ these postures as you practice telling your stories.

Although it isn't necessary to plan every movement of your body as you tell a story (just move naturally for the most part), there are some considerations to be kept in mind. If you will be performing on a stage of some sort, you will want to practice your entrance and exit. Walk confidently to the center of the stage (don't rush however) and anchor yourself in one spot. Make eye contact with all of your audience before you begin speaking. During the presentation, feel free to move about, but do so slowly and avoid losing sight of your audience. Whether you move left or right, forward or back, keep your head turned in the direction of your audience. When the performance is concluded, don't be too quick to leave the stage. Retreat slowly and confidently as the applause wanes. Again, practicing this movement prior to performance aids in establishing your confidence as a teller.

The quality of your voice distinguishes you as an individual. In general, then, you want to retain its natural pitch and tone. But there are certain aspects of your voice that may require attention. If you are soft-spoken, you will have to work to increase the volume when you perform. Similarly, if your voice is pitched quite high, you will want to work on deepening the tone. Upright posture facilitates increasing volume and lowering vocal tone by enabling you full use of your diaphragm when speaking. But the simplest way to deal with these problems is to consciously raise your volume or lower your tone as you practice telling your story.

Tailoring the Tale for Telling

Return to the original text again to sense the pace of the story and determine if anything in the story demands special body movement, gesturing, or vocal variation. You are now at the point of fine-tuning your story by tailoring it to fit your own personality.

Just as a painter begins with a blank canvas, a storyteller begins with silence. But in both arts, the conscious use of *negative space* can be very dramatic. Pausing in a story at just the right moment can heighten a sense of anticipation, signal a change of pace, or permit the audience a bit of needed relief after a particularly tense segment. In all instances, if pausing is used judiciously, it will add a most profound touch of class to your storytelling. Yet it is so easily accomplished. Look for a few spots in your story where injecting a pause would be a valuable addition and then practice telling the story with these pauses.

As with voice quality, the best rule of thumb regarding body movement and gesturing is to let it be natural. As you tell, let your hands and arms position themselves and move themselves naturally. In practice, work to discover positions that feel comfortable and natural, but don't spend an excessive amount of time as a beginner worrying about what to do with your hands, arms, and body. Now there may be a special portion of the text that necessitates a specific movement or gesture. If so, carefully plan and then practice using the gesture or movement so that the timing of its use appears natural and appropriate.

Similarly, if some aspect of the text requires special vocal treatment, plan for it carefully and practice what you have planned. In general, you will probably want to begin and end each story with a moderate volume, tone, and pace. When the situation warrants its use, increase the volume to a shout or lower it to an audible whisper. If a story increases in tension and drama, raise your pitch and volume accordingly and then lower both in the aftermath of a break point.

Putting It All Together

In summary, you want to begin your preparation by analyzing the story for its basic structure and then practice telling the story until you can deliver it with fluidity. When this is accomplished revisit the story to begin to carefully plan for and practice the incorporation of the unique touches that create personal ownership and confidence in telling the story.

Creating Performance Notes

Some storytellers find that taking notes on the analyses and tailoring decisions that have been made are important aspects of the preparation process. I find note taking particularly useful in my own preparation. Because I don't perform on a regular basis (I may not tell a story for months at a time), taking notes provides me with a handy reminder of the heart of a story and the decisions I have made to tell it. Reviewing the notes I have taken facilitates practice immediately prior to a performance because I don't have to spend countless hours reanalyzing the text.

As a suggested format, consider putting your notes on 5 × 7 index cards using the format in Fig. 7.2.

Figure 7.2

Plot Card Format

I. Bibliographic Information and/or location of the original story source:

II. Intended Audience & Rationale:

III. Personal Appeal:

IV. Average Time to Tell:

V. General Notes (Things to remember which involve the telling of the *entire* tale):

Tailoring Notes

VI. Story Introduction(s) (Write out fully):

VII. Plot Analysis (Outline Form):

    A. Exposition:

    B. Initiating Event (Plot Problem):

    C. Rising Action:

        1.   Leave the right hand

        2.   third of the card for

        etc.   tailoring notes.

    D. Climactic Event (Plot   Coordinate notes with

        Resolution):   the relevant spot in

                      the story outline.

    E. Falling Action (if any):

        1.

        2.

        etc.

    F. Ending:

The following (see Example 7.3) is a sample of notes taken for Wolkstein's (1996) "The Magic Orange Tree."

Example 7.3

<u>Analysis of "The Magic Orange Tree"</u>

I. Bibliographic Information: "The Magic Orange Tree" in *The Magic Orange Tree & Other Haitian Folktales* by Diane Wolkstein. Schocken, 1996.

II. Intended Audience & Rationale: Ages 7–8

<u>Story Element</u>	<u>Developmental Trait</u>
1. The main character is about 7–8 years old.	1. Children like hearing stories about people their own age.
2. Despite her stepmother's cruelty, Dadi fulfills the stepmother's request to make the orange tree come down because of the promise of love.	2. Children this age continue to require love & security from the family. Familial loyalty is still valued by 7–8 year olds.
3. The stepmother is disposed of in the end while Dadi is rewarded for her goodness.	3. Children this age believe in just deserts.

III. Personal Appeal:

I love the simplicity of the tale but especially the notion of childhood self-fulfillment in an adult dominated society. I am personally attracted to stories where small folks outwit larger ones as Dadi does here.

IV. Average Time to Tell: 11 min.

V. General Notes:

1. Through gesturing, locate the orange tree in a specific spot on the stage; let all other movement be related to that spot.

2. Scan audience & determine how scary to make the "arm twisting" scene.

VI. Story Introductions:

   1. Use Wolkstein's note about this
story & introduce the notion
of children in Haiti owning
a tree through the planting
of their umbilical cord with
the seed of a fruit tree.

Anchor in one spot to
begin. Pause/look at
audience before
beginning.

   2. When you were younger, did you
ever sneak cookies and get
caught by your parents?
What punishment were you
given? Could that punishment
compare to the punishment
in the story I'm about to tell you?

   3. I don't suppose anyone cares how
I got here today but I'm going
to tell you about it anyway. It
involves a story. This story!

VII. Plot Analysis:

Pause bet. Intro. &
Story.

   A. Exposition:

      Who: Dadi (hungry for love),
         Cruel stepmother.
      Where: No place specific but
         a rural setting.
      When: "Once there was a girl
         whose mother died
         the day she was born."

   B. Initiating Event (Plot Problem):

      Dadi eats stepmother's oranges;
      stepmother threatens:
      "Whoever has eaten my
      oranges had better say
      their prayers now for they'll
      not have a chance to say them
      later." (Dadi fears for her life
      at the hands of the stepmother.)

Whisper the threat in a
cruel tone of voice
(clench teeth but say
the words slowly & dis-
tinctly with intensity).

C. Rising Action:

1. Dadi runs to mother's grave; sleeps all night; wakes with renewed courage. Before going home a seed falls from her skirt & magically sprouts.	With eyes, locate spot on stage where grave & tree sprout are located.
2. Dadi sings: "Orange Tree, grow & grow & grow, Orange Tree. Orange Tree, grow & grow & grow, Orange Tree. Stepmother is not real mother, Orange Tree."	With hands held close together, gesture upward as tree trunk grows. Inject surprise & elation in voice as song is sung.
3. Dadi sings: "Orange Tree, branch & branch & branch.... "	Gesture growth, look at branching taking place.
4. Dadi sings: "Orange Tree, flower & flower & flower.... "	Gesture with hands the flowering (wide, flat hand).
5. Dadi sings: "Orange Tree, blossom & blossom & blossom.... "	Gesture with hands the blossoming (wide, rounded hand).
6. Dadi takes armful of oranges & returns home. Stepmother sees the oranges, asks where Dadi got them.	Use a sly, insincere, sugary-sweet, tone of voice.
7. Dadi doesn't tell; stepmother grabs her arm, twists, demands: "Tell Me!"	Yell "Tell me!" (if you think audience can handle a "jump tale." If not, use a deep, threatening tone of voice with intense facial expression to match.)
8. Stepmother forces Dadi to return to Orange Tree. As they approach tree,	

Dadi sings: "Orange Tree, grow & grow ... ;" tree grows out of reach.	Sing quietly but forcefully; gesture growth of tree.
9. Stepmother pleads with Dadi to make the tree come down; promises to feed/ love her as if Dadi were her own daughter.	
10. Dadi sings: "Orange Tree, lower & lower & lower ... "; tree lowers to just the right height.	Sing quietly, sorrowfully; move head up/down slowly as tree lowers into place.
11. Stepmother leaps on tree & begins to eat all the oranges. Dadi fears there will be no oranges left for her & sings: "Orange Tree, grow & grow ... ;" stepmother hangs from tree, cries for help.	Speed up the pace. Sing quickly; hand gesture growth. Gesture stepmother hanging & crying for help.
D. Climactic Event (Plot Resolution):	
Dadi sings: "Orange Tree, break & break ... ;" Tree, stepmother shatter into pieces (The stepmother is no longer a threat).	Sing loud, forcefully while pointing up at stepmother. Pause while shaking finger in the air.
E. Falling Action (if any):	
1. Dadi plants new seed & sings: "Orange Tree, grow & grow ... ;" tree grows & bears fruit.	Gesture the total growth of the tree.
2. Dadi sells oranges at the market; sells them every day for the tree is magic.	

F. Ending: I saw Dadi in the market;
asked for an orange for
free; she gave me such
a kick in the pants that
that's how I'm able to be
here to tell you the story
of the Magic Orange Tree.

DELIVERY

With the knowledge that you have prepared a story carefully and practiced what you have planned, you will have developed the confidence to tell the story to any audience. To ensure the success of your performance, there are some things that you can do before you perform and other things to keep in mind during the delivery and immediately following it.

What to Do Prior to a Performance

Unlike reading a picture book aloud, when the book should be the focus of attention, you are the attraction when telling stories. Thus, your appearance should be pleasing to your audience but not so unique so as to distract attention from the story. The situation you find yourself telling in may dictate the appropriateness of the clothing you choose to wear. You wouldn't dress the same way when telling in a classroom as opposed to telling at a summer camp. Similarly, consider wearing brighter than normal clothing when telling on a cloudy day or toning down the colors on a sunny day. The way you dress can affect the initial response of an audience to you. Colorful clothing on a cloudy day brightens the mood of your audience while moderate colors on a sunny day may have a settling effect on them.

Because performance anxiety is typically greater when telling than when reading aloud, some performers respond unconsciously by exhibiting nervous tics during a storytelling performance. You will not likely be aware of these distracting habits unless you have someone observe your performance and provide feedback to you. But once identified, you can work to eliminate these tics by consciously practicing to avoid them. One common habit is for a person to sway from side to side or back and forth as they perform. Another is to cross your legs while telling from a standing position giving the appearance that, at any moment, you may topple over. A third is to cross your arms tightly over your stomach or clasp your hands extremely tightly in front of you. Overly quick and unpredictable movement of the hands, arms, head, or entire body can also be distracting to an audience. Finally, avoiding direct eye contact with your audience and looking over or under their heads can be very distracting.

Direct eye contact is an essential aspect of the art of storytelling and is one of the elements that distinguishes storytelling from many of the other performing arts, particularly acting. As you practice telling your stories, remind yourself that storytelling is an act of communication and that your eyes meeting those of your audience is the medium for two-way interaction. Unless you break eye contact for dramatic effect, you will want to look continually into the eyes of the members of your audience. Be sure to look at everyone. It is so tempting to look only at the people directly in front of you, but the people to your left and right and to the back of your audience deserve your attention as well. As you practice your stories at home, imagine an audience before you and consciously think to make total eye contact. Also practice moving your eyes and head slowly from one person to another. Let your eye contact appear relaxed and sincere.

If you have difficulty making direct eye contact, try looking at the bridge of the noses of the members of your audience. They won't notice the difference, and you may feel a bit less anxious doing so.

If you will be performing in a setting that is new to you, make contact with the sponsor well in advance of the performance to work out the logistical details. Obviously, you will want to know the age range and any unique characteristics of your audience as well as some sense of the setting in which you will be performing. With this information, you can plan to avoid any potential problems or surprises on the day of the performance. Any special requests you may have should be communicated to the sponsor as well. If you are uncomfortable telling to auditorium-size audiences, say so and negotiate the details of telling to smaller groups, perhaps over shorter periods of time. Ask about a microphone and amplification system if telling to very large audiences, and be sure to arrive well before the performance to check out and get comfortable with the audio system and the setting in general.

Distractions during the performance should be avoided. Be willing to make suggestions regarding the performance setting to avoid them. For example, suggest changes in the seating arrangement so that the members of your audience are focused on you and away from the glare of sunlight, the movement of others nearby the performance, or extraneous noises.

Immediately prior to the performance, take the time to warm up your voice. Hum softly across the entire range of your voice. Begin talking, first at a moderate volume, then soft, then loud, and then return to a moderate volume. Take some slow, deep breaths to relax.

What to Do During the Performance

There are three basic things to remember to do during the performance: Enjoy the experience, keep eye contact with your audience, and just let the stories happen. If you have prepared well, you will accomplish all three tasks because you will have developed the confidence to trust yourself, the story, and the collaborative interaction with the audience, which will bring the story to life.

THE QUESTION OF ETHICS

There is much debate currently taking place that involves the responsibility of storytellers to those people (sometimes other tellers) who have provided the sources of the stories they are telling. In the absence of any laws for storytelling comparable to copyright laws for print material, the debate has focused on the issue of ethics. For beginning tellers, with any story you learn, it will likely be the case that your first version of the story will be quite similar to the version that serves as your source. But as you continue to tell the story, if you are avoiding, as recommended, word-for-word recitation, you will find that your version changes and, at some point, becomes perceptibly (perhaps completely) different than the original. Certainly, when you first start telling the story in public, as a matter of courtesy, you should always cite the source of the tale. Moreover, if you are an educator or librarian, you want to introduce any printed form of a story you've told primarily as a means of encouraging members of your audience to read the text for themselves. Even later when your version of a story has changed substantially from the original, I believe that it is a matter of courtesy to credit the source of your inspiration.

The issue of telling stories from cultures (including ethnic, religious, gender, etc.) other than your own is even more problematic and cloudy than that of telling stories or versions of stories that were first developed by other tellers or authors. Some folks believe that there should be strict prohibitions in this regard and that nobody should tell a story unless he or she is of the culture from which the story originated. By contrast, others feel that the notion of ownership of stories in the oral tradition is universal and, therefore, that all stories should be available for telling by all tellers. Personally, I take a moderate stance on the issue. Recall my comments in chapter 6 on the value of storytelling with regard to acculturation and tolerance of others. I believe that it is possible to gain a deeper and fuller understanding of others through story—not only by reacting to stories from other cultures, but by creating them as well. Many authors and storytellers have developed or delivered authentic stories with characters from cultures other than their own. But the authenticity of their creations is the result, to a great extent, of their having developed a thorough understanding of the other culture and a sensitivity to any prohibitions that culture places on those stories or the processes by which they are shared with others., It seems to me that all storytellers have the responsibility to understand and honor the cultural traditions surrounding the stories they choose to tell.

For more definitive directives with regard to citing sources, gaining permission from the originator of a tale for purposes of recording or publishing a tale, telling tales from other cultures, or a general discussion of the topic of ethics in storytelling, you should refer to Klein's (1999) extensive article entitled "Ethics, Apprenticeship, Etiquette, Courtesy, and Copyright" or three specific editions of *Storytelling Magazine* (National Storytelling Association).

EXTENDED PRACTICE ACTIVITIES

Developmental Activities

1. Share your feelings about telling stories to live audiences with other beginning storytellers.

2. Survey your read-aloud repertoire to determine whether there are any stories that you could easily tell without looking at the text. In private, try telling these selected stories out loud. Don't worry about word-for-word accuracy. Feel free to vary the nonessential elements of the text.

3. In a group of one or two peers, try telling *The Surprise* (Shannon, 1983) with no preparation. Note how each telling varies from one person to the next.

4. From published sources (texts, tape recordings, records, etc.), create a list of two or more tales that are 2-minute tales for you. Discuss these tales with a small group of peers. Be able to justify to them why these stories are appropriate 2-minute tales for you. Tell a tale or two with little or no preparation to demonstrate that they are 2-minute tales.

Culminating Activity

Thoroughly prepare a story for telling and then perform it for an appropriate live audience.

RESOURCES

Handy Sources of Two-Minute Tales

de Spain, P. (1994). *Twenty-two splendid tales to tell from around the world* (Vol. I and II). Little Rock, AR: August House Publishers.

Holt, D., & Mooney, B. (1994). *Ready-to-tell tales*. Little Rock, AR: August House Publishers.

MacDonald, M. R. (1986). *Twenty tellable tales: Audience participation folktales for the beginning storyteller*. New York: H. W. Wilson Company.

Partial List of Storytelling Support Groups

NSN (National Storytelling Network), 116 ½ West Main St., Jonesborough, TN 37659, (800) 525–4514. (Former Names: the National Storytelling Membership Association, the National Storytelling Association, the National Association for the Preservation & Perpetuation of Storytelling)

International Order of EARS. Inc., 12019 Donohue Ave., Louisville, KY 40243, (502) 245–0643.

8

Telling Your Own
Self-Created Tales

Self-created tales can take a variety of forms but all hold in common the fact that you are the original author. Narratives created by prominent authors fall into this category as well. Some of these authors who are also storytellers in the traditional sense craft their stories in oral form to be told to audiences and simultaneously or subsequently publish them in print form to be enjoyed by audiences via reading. These stories can fall into any of the standard genres of narrative except, of course, for traditional literature where the original authorship is unknown. With traditional literature, however, many professional storytellers spend months researching a particular folk tale and then create their own unique variant of it. In these instances, the author, in truth, is designated as the *reteller* but the process of creation is quite similar to that followed by the author of an original story.

Another subcategory of the self-created tale is variously named the *autobiographical tale*, *personal narrative*, or *family story*. Here the characters and settings in the story are real people known to the author (including oneself) who are either living or were once alive.

For you as a beginning teller, the beauty of taking the time to create a story from scratch is that the memory work required to learn to tell it is much easier than learning to tell someone else's story. This is so either because the memorizing of the plot structure is completed during the creation of the story or, as in the case of a personal story, the plot, setting, and characters are already well known to you. Moreover, because you have much greater personal investment in this type of tale, it will likely result in a livelier telling on your part than the telling of another's story.

There are, however, drawbacks in developing a self-created story. The crafting of the story adds an additional step to the preparation process—the creation of the story, which may take considerable time to complete, not to mention the mental work required to find a good story to tell in the first place. In addition, stories you create yourself must have some universal truth in them. Otherwise, they will be of little interest to anyone but you and, thus, not worth sharing with an audience. Moreover, a major risk in self-created stories, particularly for the beginner, is that they tend to ramble. To avoid these pitfalls, then, steps must be taken in the preparation process to discover thematic richness in your story material and to impose a tight narrative structure on the events that constitute your plot. Whatever struggling may be necessary to craft your own stories, the time spent doing so will be worth all your effort in the long run. Many professional storytellers believe that the kind of self-discovery one experiences when one crafts one's own stories is a necessary part of the journey to becoming a true artist (Klein, 1999, pp. 8–9).

SELECTION

With self-created stories, the selection process involves locating material from which a story can be created. You may be aware that stories often share archetypal motifs (e.g., "the underdog," "the quest," and "rags to riches"). You can create stories using these motifs as the foundation for your stories. Sometimes the seed of a story can be found in other types of literature such as newspaper articles, songs, jokes, or poems. Photographs too can be a rich source of potential story material (see Provenzo, Provenzo, & Zorn, 1984). But an unbelievable wealth of material is most likely located close to home—in your own memory. The problem here involves retrieval. All too frequently, I have heard my graduate storytelling students state that nothing interesting has ever happened in their lives. Chance alone dictates that this is hardly possible. But retrieving gems from your past is difficult without the help of some sort of aid to facilitate your remembering. Family photographs, keepsakes, letters, and diaries can be of use here.

Steve Zeitlin is a folklorist who has studied family stories for some time now. He and his research colleagues have discovered that there are commonly shared motifs in these stories just as there are in all types of literature (Zeitlin, Kotkin, & Baker, 1982). Utilizing these motifs, you can search through your past experience and discover relevant anecdotes that may hold great potential for story material. As a suggestion, begin to make a list of the anecdotes you remember by using a word or phrase that readily reminds you of the incident. Avoid deselecting any anecdote because you think it is inconsequential. On later reflection, you may discover that it holds some value or that

Figure 8.1
Motifs
Types of People: heroes, innocents, rogues, mischief makers, neighborhood ogres, bratty kids, practical jokers, survivors, unique personalities
Interpersonal relations: sibling rivalries, family feuds, rituals, family secrets, unique sayings, unique names, superstitions, blind dates, courtships
Momentous events: lost fortunes (big or small), lost artifacts (keys, wedding rings), embarrassing moments, accidents or near-accidents, mistakes, celebrations, childhood crushes, migrations, vacations, firsts/lasts, dreams, wishes, supernatural happenings
Unique settings: home, amusement parks, vacation spots, haunted spots, memorable places
Artifacts: childhood toys or dolls, keepsakes, photographs, pets, special clothes
Emotions: mosts (when were you the most jealous, angry, sad, happy, scared, etc.)

it, in combination with other anecdotes, exposes a pattern in your life that could be the basis for a story. The list of motifs above (see Fig. 8.1) includes those derived by Zeitlin et al. plus others that I have discovered in working with my graduate storytelling students. Feel free to augment this list with motifs that characterize your life. Using this list, think back through your past life and brainstorm for anecdotes related to these motifs. Example 8.1 is a sample list of relevant anecdotes from my past life.

Example 8.1

Craig's List

Motif	Anecdote
Innocents:	Jimmy Joyce (a nice kid who just wanted a friend)
Mischief Makers:	Me (I continually made Jimmy Joyce's life miserable)
Heroes:	Johnny Roe (the day he helped me when I broke my leg)
	Roberto Clemente
	SiHugo Green

Unique characters:	Uncle Kate Uncle Louie Jim F.
Memorable Places:	Kennywood Park Uncle Louie's farm on Lake Erie St. Bernard's Elementary School
Names:	The Krugh's had nicknames for every kid in the neighborhood
Family Feuds:	Brother John & his toy soldiers, model planes
Unique sayings:	"Sawzie Dusties" "Dinky" "You'ns"
Accidents:	Flight to the Philippines Nathaniel meets the fire hydrant
Firsts:	First love—Carla M. First date—M.
Mosts:	Sad—Scuffy Cut from the Pirates Happy—Christmases as a kid Community Picnic Day Scared—Stuck on a mountain
Mistakes:	"You missed it" "Menos ka!"

Keep a running list of anecdotes and revise and review them from time to time. Look for any interconnections between anecdotes and attempt to identify any significant themes in the anecdotes or interconnections. Refer to chapter 2 for guidelines for abstracting themes. This identification will enable you to determine, in part, which material has the potential to be transformed into a self-constructed story that will be of interest to an audience beyond yourself.

PREPARATION

You have become familiar with the structure of a narrative and have experience analyzing a story into its constituent narrative parts. Creating your self-constructed stories involves applying this analysis process in the reverse. With a motif, anecdote, or set of anecdotes that you have determined to have thematic significance to others, you can now begin crafting your story by imposing narrative structure onto the story material. Thus, you will be crafting an exposition, initiating event (being certain to clearly identify the plot problem), rising action, climactic event (with the plot resolution), any falling action if necessary, and an ending. This process is most crucial in your preparation to avoid a story that lacks direction—one that audiences will find boring or unpredictable and confusing. As a preliminary exercise in developing the crafting process, try your hand at the exercise in Fig. 8.2.

Different people work in different ways when constructing a story, but I would recommend that you write out the story completely while segmenting it, at some point, into the various narrative parts. (An example of this format is provided in chapter 7 using Galdone's *The Three Billy Goats Gruff*.)

One comment must be made at this point. In constructing your story into a fully formed narrative, you must not be afraid to fabricate plot elements that may never have actually happened even though the story may be about

---

Figure 8.2

Story Construction From a Plot Motif

Directions:	Using the following plot motif and plot questions construct the rudiments of a story to be told to children.
Plot Motif:	A young lonely child in the absence of any real friends creates and interacts with an imaginary friend. The child insists that other real humans in his midst acknowledge the reality of the imaginary friend by requesting, for example, that a place be set at the dinner table for the imaginary friend.
Plot Questions:	What is the child's name? What is the setting (time/place)? What observable behavior of both the child and/or others around him/her indicate that the child is lonely?
	How is the imaginary friend introduced to the world?
	What are the observable behaviors of the child interacting with his imaginary friend?
	Does the imaginary friend eventually disappear? How? Why? As a result of what events? Is this a necessary conclusion to the story? How else could it end?

real people and events. Remember that the real truth of a story is located in its thematic structure not in the plot (for more information on the concept of *truth* in personal stories, refer to Davis, 1993, p. 7). Feel free then to invent characters, scenes, and events to adequately deliver the thematic truth to your audience. If you have used the actual names of real people in your story and are not comfortable attributing self-created personality traits or behaviors to them (or, for that matter, actual ones) to complete the narrative, simply change the names of your characters or their relationship to you. A valuable story about your brother could just as easily be attributed to a distant relative or friend. Or you could tell the story in the third person as if the story characters have no relationship to you at all.

To begin the crafting, mentally describe the story setting in detail. You may not necessarily expose the full description in your actual story but it's a good idea to have a fully formed sense of place throughout the construction of the story. Do the same with your characters. In both cases, apply all the senses in creating your descriptions. How do things sound, look, feel, smell, or taste? How do characters look, move, talk, and behave? What clothes do they typically wear? What is the color of their skin, eyes, and hair? What makes their mannerism or behavior unique? Let your setting and characters be personally familiar to you. Then, with these images in mind, begin to create an exposition but be sparing in description. Throughout the story, expose only those images that further the progression of the plot.

Once you have a basic sense of the exposition, clearly and specifically identify the initiating event and plot problem. At this point, it may also be helpful if you identify the climactic event and resolution, although some people prefer to let the drama of the story evolve through the writing. But identifying the problem and resolution immediately may give you an added sense of security and a clearer sense of direction in forming the plot. Begin to add elements of the rising action that heighten the suspense created with the plot problem. Again, be sparing in construction by keeping your major theme and the plot problem-resolution relationship constantly in mind as the leavening agent. With the climactic moment identified, ask yourself if any loose ends in the plot need to be cared for. If so, tie them up in a brief falling action. If not, complete the text with a short ending.

For alternative strategies for developing self-created stories, consult Dixon's (1992) "Storytelling World Presents: Donald Davis," Davis' (1993) *Telling Your Own Stories*, and Joy's (1997) "Creating and Crafting Stories." Information for creating historical stories can be found in the Summer/Fall edition of *Storytelling World* (Joy, 1992) as well as one article by Elizabeth Ellis in the Winter/Spring 1997 edition (Joy, 1997). "Multicultural Storytelling" is the topic under consideration in the Summer/Fall 1994 issue of

Storytelling World (Joy, 1994). If you want to add sound effects to your story, consult Petersen (1995). If you want to inject humor, check the Summer/Fall 1993 issue of *Storytelling World* (Joy, 1997) particularly Petersen's article "Seven Ways to Add Humor to Your Story" on pp. 15–17.

Expect revision. As you begin to practice telling your story, you'll vary parts of the original text to feel more natural in the oral form—a perfectly normal progression. As always is the case with any told story, its form will change from one telling to the next. The likelihood is that you will find that bringing your self-constructed stories to life is much easier than with stories that others have created. Use this relative comfort then to work on improving your tailoring techniques.

Some stories that you create will be highly emotional for you, but you can't let yourself become overly emotional while performing the story. As such, you'll have to establish some distance between you and the story before attempting to perform it. One way to do this is to practice telling the story in private for many more times than is necessary to establish basic fluidity in your telling. In this way, you will develop a certain numbness toward the story content that will enable you to perform it without becoming overly emotional.

For note-taking purposes it might be easier to use standard writing or typing paper than note cards because you will want to include the entirety of the text you have created. Use the format in Fig. 8.3 for these notes. You may want to protect your self-created stories by establishing copyright. Contact the Register of Copyright, Library of Congress, Washington, DC 20559, for information regarding the process for formally applying for copyright. Also consult "Copyright Issues for Storytellers" (Kevin, 1996).

SAMPLE STORY

"Jimmy Joyce and the Lesson Well Learned" is a personal story that I created some years ago. The original idea came as a result of brainstorming personal anecdotes using the Zeitlin rubric introduced previously in this chapter. You will note from my previous list of anecdotes that Jimmy Joyce appears as an "innocents" anecdote and that I appear as a "mischief maker." In truth, as a mischievous 9-year-old, I was quite mean to Jimmy, who was a nice boy my age who simply needed a friend. I can't recount the particular things I did to Jimmy but I do remember that I was always nasty to him. So not all the things I attribute as happening to Jimmy in the story actually took place. If memory serves me well, Jimmy was actually the boy on the tricycle and it was my father who saved him that day. But I didn't push him out of his driveway. I think he just lost control of the trike himself. My brother and I did tie Jimmy up in our garage but my mother caught us doing it almost immediately. I did

---

Figure 8.3

Format for Note Taking
Storytelling of a Self-Constructed Story

Using standard typing paper provide the following information:

I. Story Title:

II. Author, Date Constructed/Revised:

III. Intended Audience:

IV. Rationale:

V. Personal Appeal:

VI. Themes (List several significant ones):

VII. Time:Introduction- Story-

VIII. General Notes (Things to remember that involve the telling
of the entire tale & not specific to any one segment of the telling):

                                                          Tailoring Notes
IX. Introduction(s) (Write out fully):

X. Plot Analysis (Write out the text fully but divide it into the
following segments):

   A. Exposition:

   B. Initiating Event (Plot Problem):

   C. Rising Action
      1.
      2.
      3.
      Etc.   (Leave the right-
                                         hand third of the
   D. Climactic Event (Plot Resolution):   page for tailoring
                                         notes. Coordinate with
   E. Falling Action (if any):   the relevant spot in
      1.   the story where the
      2.
      etc.   tailoring occurs.)

   F. Ending:

---

trip Jimmy (at least once) as I describe in the story, and he did, in fact, return
the favor. In reality, I was the kid whose head was painted (and Ray Fream
and my brother actually did the painting). I did throw a house brick at some
other kid once but in retaliation for equally nasty things he'd done to me.
Still and all, in my meanness toward Jimmy, I conceivably could have actually done everything to him that I set out in the story. To this day, however,
what I retain most clearly from it all is a sense of regret. So my telling of the

story today serves as an apology to Jimmy and a thank you, as well, for the valuable lesson he unknowingly taught me.

The story has been revised countless times since its inception. Two additions, the reference to Kennywood Park/community picnic day and the *dinky*, were added after reviewing my list of anecdotes (i.e., "Memorable Places," "Unique Sayings," and "Mosts"). The following notes (see Example 8.2) utilize the format introduced in Fig. 8.3.

DELIVERY

Example 8.2

Sample Notes Taken for the Self-Constructed Story Entitled "Jimmy Joyce & the Lesson Well Learned"

I. Story Title: Jimmy Joyce & the Lesson Well Learned

II. Author, Date Constructed/Revised: R. Craig Roney 11/20/77
Major Revisions: 11/26/77, 4/6/83, 9/2/94

III. Intended Audience:
A. 9–11 year olds
B. Adults

IV. Rationale:

Story Element (For 9–11 year olds)	Developmental Trait
1. The main characters are about 9 years old.	1. Children like hearing stories about people their own age.
2. Jimmy is a victim of injustice.	2. Children this age can empathize with someone who suffers injustice.
3. Much of the humor in the story is overt & broad but the humor at the end of the story is more subtle involving word play and irony.	3. Fourth-Sixth graders are extending their appreciation of humor beyond the purely physical to include word play.

(For Adults)

| 1. The story is told from an adult perspective ("But from that day to this one, I'll never forget ... " | 1. Adults like hearing stories about other adults. |
| 2. There is a sense of regret on the part of the adult narrator. | 2. Regret is an emotion most commonly associated with adults. |

V. Personal Appeal: I've come to appreciate the lessons in life I learned as a child. Reflecting on these lessons has helped me to more clearly define who I am today.

VI. Themes: What goes around, comes around.
Don't be surprised if others treat you the way you have treated them.
Some things have to be learned the hard way.

VII. Time: Introduction—11 sec.
Story—6½ min.

VIII. General Things To Remember:
Avoid getting so involved in the story that you forget the audience. Watch carefully their (esp. adults) reaction to the initial incidents and lighten the tone or get through the story quickly if the reaction is negative.

Tailoring Notes

IX. Introduction:
All things change. All things have a beginning and an ending. This story is about one such beginning and ending; about a change and the lesson that I learned from it.

X. Plot Analysis
A. Exposition:
My family lived on a hill. Actually we lived at the bottom of it. A

street ran down the middle of the
hill. It was a brick street, quite
bumpy and difficult to negotiate
on a tricycle or wagon. There were
houses on both sides of the street.
And on the north side, at the top of
the hill in between each of the
houses, there were steep embankments that ran down to the top of a
concrete retaining wall which
extended the length of a second
street. This street angled into our own
merging together in front of the
apartment where my family lived.
The retaining wall was about 5' high for
most of its length. There was a sidewalk beside the wall, then the street
and then the streetcar tracks. The
streetcar, we used to call it the
"dinky."

Our street usually bustled with
activity due, in part, to the large
number of kids living in the
neighborhood. And all of the kids
lived at the bottom of the hill,
all except Jimmy.

Initiating Event:

He lived at the top of the hill and
you'd think he'd have learned to
stay out of our part of the neighborhood. You'd think he'd have
learned to run away when he saw us
coming up into his part. You'd think
he'd have learned to stay away from
me and my older brother, Johnny,
and Ray Fream. (Jimmy never seemed
to learn from his experiences)

Margin notes:

May mention it
was LeMoyne
Ave., may
describe brick.

Use hands to
indicate how
steep.

Don't pause

Rising Action:

1. Especially Ray. After all, it was Ray
who covered Jimmy's head with red   Pick up pace.
house paint, then ran to tell Jimmy's
Aunt Martha that Jimmy'd sliced his
head open. Now Aunt Martha sure
screamed a lot when she saw Jimmy.
But, in the end, it was Jimmy who
screamed the loudest because he had
to suffer through a painful head washing
process. And, besides, he got an awful
spanking from his uncle to boot.   Pause, slow pace.

2. And you'd think Jimmy'd have learned
to avoid Johnny and me—especially after
that day we'd played cowboys and Indians
with him. We really didn't mean to tie
Jimmy up and leave him in our garage
for six or seven hours. But tying Jimmy up
seemed to be the most exciting part of
playing cowboys and Indians that morning.
And after we'd done it and hightailed it out
of the garage, we sort of lost interest in
playing that game and sort of forgot about Jimmy.

Now Jimmy was a crybaby and it's a good
thing he was. If my mother hadn't heard
him crying out in the garage, he might
have missed breakfast the next morning
instead of lunch and dinner the way it was.

3. Anyway, you'd think Jimmy'd have
learned. You'd think he'd have learned to
stay away from somebody like me; someone
who had hit him in the head with a house
brick one time. Someone who had coaxed
him onto a tricycle then pushed him out of
his driveway and watched him tear down
our brick street, out of control, yelling and
screaming all the way to the bottom of the
hill. It was fortunate for Jimmy that my
dad saw him coming and yanked him off

the trike before he got to the intersection
of the street and the dinky tracks.

4. As you might guess, I could never understand why Jimmy liked me and wanted
to be my friend. You'd think he'd have   Pause
learned.

We weren't at all alike. Jimmy was large
for his age; big, slow moving, and
awkward. I, on the other hand, was
very small and thin, but quick, and
agile. I had to be quick to keep from
getting caught.

My parents took Johnny and me
to lots of interesting places. Jimmy
didn't have parents. Someone said
that they'd been killed in a car
accident. So Jimmy lived with his aunt
and uncle who weren't used to kids and
rarely took Jimmy anywhere of interest
to us kids. So Jimmy and I really didn't
have too much to talk about.

I couldn't understand why Jimmy wanted
to be my friend. You'd think he'd have
learned!

5. One day Jimmy and I were playing at
the top of one of those embankments that
separated the houses up our street. We
were between the Rayburns and
Tharansky's houses and we'd been
standing there watching for the dinky
to pass by. For some strange reason, I
tripped Jimmy and watched him roll
down the embankment and over the
top of the retaining wall. When he hit
the sidewalk below, he must have
hurt himself because he started to
cry. Well I didn't like crybabies, so I
went home.

The very next day, Jimmy and I were playing in his yard and I said: "Hey Jimmy, let's go over to Rayburn's and watch for the dinky." Jimmy agreed so we walked over to the top of the embankment. When we'd been there for a few minutes, I tripped Jimmy again and he rolled down the embankment and over the wall again. But I went home because Jimmy started crying again.

Now I didn't see Jimmy the next day. That's because it was community picnic day when everybody went to Kennywood Park to ride the roller-coasters. I don't imagine Jimmy got to go so I didn't see him that day. But I did see him the next day. And we went to the Rayburn's again, and I tripped Jimmy again. I guess I must have tripped Jimmy like that seven or eight times and then tripping him got sort of boring so I stopped seeing him. And you'd think he'd have learned!   Pause

6. You can imagine my surprise when, three months later, Jimmy came down into our part of the neighborhood. And when he saw me he said: "Hey, Craig. Want to play?" And I said: "Ya! Let's go watch for the dinky up at Rayburn's." And Jimmy agreed.

When we got to the top of the embank-   Show with
ment, I set Jimmy up just where I   hands &
wanted him. Then I tried to trip him ...   body
but I couldn't do it.   positioning

Climactic Event:

Then Jimmy tripped me and I went rolling down the embankment and over the wall. And when I hit the sidewalk, I

hurt my knee, my elbow, and my head.
And I started crying and yelling all at
once. (As it turns out, Jimmy did learn
from his experiences)

Falling Action:

Then I leaped up that wall and tore up
that embankment yelling and screaming
all the way: "I'll teach you, Jimmy
Joyce! I'll teach you!" But when I got
to the top, Jimmy had vanished.

And I guess I did teach Jimmy a lesson
that day.

Ending:

I never saw him again. He moved away
from our neighborhood some days later.
But from that day to this very day, I'll
always remember Jimmy Joyce and the
lesson well learned.

You need not make any changes in the way you deliver a self-constructed story relative to any other type of told story. But because this is a story you have created, there may be the tendency to gloat on it or oversell it in an introduction or follow-up to the telling. Be careful to avoid this pitfall. If the story is well constructed and has thematic richness, it can stand on its own merit.

EXTENDED PRACTICE ACTIVITIES

Developmental Activities

1. Generate a list of anecdotes from your past life using the guidelines from Fig. 8.1. With your list, note any interconnections among anecdotes and attempt to identify significant themes related to the anecdotes singly or in combination. You might find that this process works better if you do it in pairs or even in a small group. Listing to others sharing their anecdotes will often stimulate your own memory.

2. Choose one of the following exercises to complete (see Figs. 8.4 and 8.5).

3. Choose an anecdote (or combination of anecdotes) from the list created in Activity 1. Try constructing the rudiments of a story by following a process

---

Figure 8.4

Story Construction From a Plot Motif

Directions: Using the following plot motif and plot questions construct the rudiments
   of a story to be told to teenagers.

Plot Motif: A teenager decides to run away from home.

Plot Questions: What is the teen's name? What is the setting (time/place)?

   What provoked the teen to make the decision to run away?

   What preparations (if any) does the teen make to run away?

   Does the teen carry out the decision? If not, why? What event stopped the teen? If so, how far
      does the teen go? Does he/she return home? What are the circumstances?

   How does the story end?

Figure 8.5

Story Construction From a Plot Motif

Directions: Using the following plot motif and plot questions construct the rudiments
   of a story to be told to adults.

Plot Motif: A braggart is challenged by peers into making good on an outrageous boast.

Plot Questions: What is the braggart's name? What does he/she
   look like? How old is he/she? Has he/she always been a
   braggart? What is the setting (time/place)?

   What is the boast? How does the braggart get trapped into the challenge?

   Does the braggart get out of this tough situation? How?

---

similar to the one you followed in Activity 2 (you'll have to create your own plot
questions, which will vary from one anecdote to another).

   4. If you skipped reading chapter 5, return to it and read the section on creating a wordless picture book story. Then try your hand at Developmental Activities 1 and 2 and Culminating Activity 1 at the end of that chapter. These
activities will be beneficial in helping you develop stories from scratch.

Culminating Activity

Create your own story and then share it with an appropriate audience.

RESOURCES

Pellowski, A. (1987). *The family storytelling handbook*. New York: Macmillan.

PART IV

DEVELOPING STORY
PERFORMANCE
PROGRAMS

9

Creating a Story Performance Program

There may be times when you want to string together the performance of several stories in a sequence. Whether the stories are read aloud, told, or a combination of the two performance modes, careful thought must be given to the development of the program beyond the basic concerns discussed in previous chapters.

SELECTION

Whether the program is to be performed in an environment with which you are very familiar or one that you don't know well, your programmatic decision making (particularly the selection of the stories to be performed) will be easier if you gather preliminary information about the setting in which you will be performing. What will be the size of the audience? Who will be the members of the audience (consider age, gender, special needs)? If children, what are their names and are there any names with unique pronunciations? What will be the seating arrangement? Is the setting unique in any way? (Will the performance be outdoors, in an auditorium or small room? Is the setting in a high-traffic area or next to open windows close by a playground where distractions are likely? Is the backdrop for the performer likely to be distracting?) Will you need special equipment or arrangements (e.g., microphone, overhead projector, clock that you can easily see, table, chair, or stool)? What is the purpose of the program? (Is there an identifiable theme for the program?) Knowing the answers to these questions will enable you to make story selection and other decisions beforehand to ensure that the performance runs as smoothly as possible. Be careful not to treat lightly a setting that is familiar to you. Take the time to think through the relationship between this setting and the stories you plan to perform—a good way to avoid any surprises during the performance that could undermine its effectiveness.

WORKING WITH VARIED AUDIENCES

Preschool children tend to be the most unpredictable of all audiences. Although some young children have had lots of experience as members of an audience, it's best to assume that most youngsters this age are new to story performance programs and, therefore, don't yet know what behavior is expected. Typically, these children are egocentric and literal-minded, have short attention spans, and are quite active, interactive, and imaginative.

Beyond the obvious need to choose stories of high interest to these young children, consider keeping your stories and the program brief. A program of 15 to 20 minutes is sufficient (shorter if the audience is large or if the logistics of the environment prevent you from getting sufficiently close to your audience to be able to better control them through your presence and the stories being performed). Simply being close by is enough to control most children. However, if necessary, you can gently touch the shoulder of a child to regain lost attention. If possible, have the children wear name tags that you can readily see during the performance so that you can inject a child's name into the fabric of the story you're telling—a great way to personalize a story and subtly control inappropriate behavior. Include at least one interactive story or poem that engages the children more physically than simply listening, and be prepared to substitute more active stories for the ones you originally planned if the children get restless early in the program.

Avoid asking rhetorical questions of these children (the questions will be taken literally) and, for any questions you ask, know that the children will likely respond openly to them. Becoming sidetracked from your program is always a concern here so carefully consider the questions, if any, that you ask and be prepared to use children's responses to get back on track. This requires that you listen carefully to what the children say and think on your feet. Be prepared for surprises but avoid stopping the story to respond to a child's spontaneous verbal reactions to some part of the story. Learn to cultivate the art of judiciously ignoring this behavior, and try your best to keep the flow of a story and the program going.

Some less experienced audiences of primary grade children may react to stories similarly to preschoolers and so must be dealt with in similar fashion.

But because of their maturity, these children typically can sit through longer stories and programs (a half hour is a good time frame). With more time available, you can inject greater variety into the program, blending telling and reading aloud together in a single sitting. Children this age still enjoy participation stories but the stories have to match their level of sophistication, and your means of presentation has to avoid condescension. These children don't deserve to be treated as babies. But they can get restless, so you'd be wise to have handy a brief song, poem, finger play, or relief activity that gets them up and moving about in between stories. By contrast, you want to be careful with *scary* material. These children like to be scared through a story but the person performing must be someone they trust would never harm them. Thus, if your audience is not familiar with you, use scary stories judiciously.

Upper elementary audiences, especially ones with much experience as an audience, are generally easy to perform for. With maturity, they know what behavior is expected of them and they are capable of sitting through longer and more sophisticated stories and programs. These children can easily handle programs lasting from one half hour to 45 minutes; they can even sit through a single told story that lasts that long or deal with excerpts read to them from lengthier stories.

The biggest challenge for a performer, particularly a storyteller, when working with adolescents is to win their trust. Unfortunately, most teens have developed a negative image of storytelling, considering it babyish. Moreover, they are easily embarrassed and are at a point in their lives where they tend to distance themselves from adults, especially ones who appear not to act their age or who seem to want to lecture them. Thus, they consider storytelling to be childish or overly didactic and listening to a storyteller to be embarrassing. When asked to attend a storytelling program, they tend to throw up a variety of defense mechanisms that interfere with the interaction between teller and audience, which is so vital to the success of a storytelling performance. With adolescent audiences, then, it is important to win their trust (or at least their attention) with the first story in your program. One way to do this is to choose either a very serious and mature story to begin or a good (and mature) ghost or scary story. Save the humor, romance, or embarrassing moments stories for later in the program when, having won this special audience's trust, you can afford to share with them stories that engage them in the exploration of the more sensitive or vulnerable issues in their lives. When choosing stories for the entire program, it is vitally important with teens that you choose ones that meet their more mature needs and interests—no time for fairy godmother stories or stories delivered in a syrupy voice.

Adults, arguably, are the easiest audiences for whom to perform. Although you may be more apprehensive about playing to adults than to children, it is important to remember that the behavior of an adult audience is almost completely predictable and supportive of the performer. Moreover, adults will tolerate virtually any type of story, although they may be disappointed if a performer should choose children's stories when adult stories were expected. Even in this case, adults usually behave civilly during a performance, unlike young children who may act inappropriately if the performer's stories aren't to their liking. Elderly audiences can be unpredictable. Some may appear quite passive, even inattentive, whereas others may seem disruptive. Typically, however, these audiences are very appreciative and attuned to the performer's stories. Consider providing time for these folks to share their stories with you after you have shared your stories with them.

Mixed audiences present a unique challenge to the performer. With mixed ages of children, you have to continually keep in mind the needs of the youngest of your audience members otherwise you may lose their interest and they, in turn, may become disruptive. If at all possible, avoid audiences of children with large age spans. It isn't a good idea to perform for middle-school students together with preschoolers, for example. Beforehand, try scheduling for these two groups separately and avoid the problem altogether. But if you have no choice and must perform for child audiences that vary greatly in age, try to choose stories that are broad in appeal. Begin your program with a story that meets the needs of the youngest children in the audience and always follow up a story for the oldest children with one that is attractive to the youngest ones. Also try to keep the more mature stories as short as possible, and limit the length of the program so that it doesn't extend beyond the attention span of the youngest children. It's better to leave the more mature children hungry for more good story performances than to risk overextending the younger ones.

With adults and children mixed together, you can gear all your stories to the children and not worry that the adults will become bored. In this setting, the adults will expect children's stories and enjoy them as such. In organizing the audience, consider having the children sit beside their parents rather than separated from them. In this way, the parents can control the behavior of their children (so that you don't have to) and can model for their children (especially the very young ones) appropriate audience behavior—a good learning experience.

BALANCING STORIES READ AND STORIES TOLD

A program can consist entirely of stories read aloud or stories told or can be a mix of both modes of performance. There are no hard and fast rules here.

Your decision as to which option to choose should be based on the needs and interests of your audience. Brightly colored picture books gain the attention of very young children so you might choose to read one after telling a story to this age audience. Following the telling of a complex story to teens, you might choose to read a brief excerpt from a book that further exemplifies a concept originally exposed in the told story. If your program has a particular theme and your repertoire of told stories relative to that theme is limited, complete the program by adding read-alouds.

STORY PERFORMANCE IN THE SCHOOL CURRICULUM

As stated in chapters 1 and 6, children benefit in a variety of ways from listening to stories read and told to them. This benefit doesn't stop when children enter school. Educators must continue performing stories for children to reinforce and extend the attitudes and skills they need to become truly literate. But to be effective, the performance of stories must become a regular, ongoing part of the school day. Reading and telling stories to children on an occasional basis will have little effect on their development As such, teachers must consciously plan for the incorporation of reading aloud and storytelling into the curriculum on a daily basis.

PREPARATION

Sequencing Stories in a Program

In general, with programs that involve two or more stories, consider providing audiences with at least one humorous story and one that creates some serious food for thought. But let the sequence of stories vary depending on the make-up of the specific audience. As mentioned earlier, with teen audiences, I prefer to start with something serious to win their trust. Once done, I can afford to lighten the atmosphere with a humorous tale. With primary grade children, I reverse this order because I can grab their attention best by sharing a funny story first. Then, with their attention in hand, I can expect that they will continue to attend as I share something more serious with them.

With more complex programs involving many stories, the sequence of presentation can be based on each story's length and tone, the medium of presentation used, whether the story involves more active participation by the audience, and the content of each story. In this latter instance, if you think carefully about each story you plan to perform (or have available to perform), you usually can discover a natural interrelationship between them and then base your sequencing and your program introduction, transitions from one story to the next, ending, and follow-up activity on that interrelationship. In some instances, you may wish to identify a concept or theme to serve as the unifying element for a program. In recent years, for example, I have performed programs for a local middle school on the concept of *Colonial Storytelling* (to tie into an eighth-grade unit on that historical period) and one on *bullies* (because the teachers felt the need to address a bully problem they were having in the school).

As a general rule of thumb, sequence your stories to provide variety (thus to generate and maintain interest by the audience); a long story followed by a short one, a serious story followed by a humorous one, a story that involves active participation by the audience followed by one that simply requires the audience to relax and listen, a told story followed by something read aloud, a poem followed by a narrative. Utilizing mediated storytelling can spice up any performance.

Program Introductions, Transitions, and Endings

Before beginning your performance, you need to settle the audience into a listening mode and, especially if the audience doesn't know you well, introduce yourself and your program. At the program's conclusion, you need to provide the audience with some sense of finality and closure. Throughout the performance, programmatic flow can be created by providing transitions from one story to another.

Many tellers use stock introductions and endings, often choosing poems such as Shel Silverstein's (1974) "Invitation" or Laura Simms' "Turkish Storyteller's Poem" (Livo, 1983) for such purposes. Still others employ ritual beginnings and endings such as lighting and extinguishing a story candle or, for very young children, pantomiming the imposition and removal of *listening ears*. Transitions typically involve your saying something that relates the previous story or poem to that which is to follow, but can also involve the use of artifacts that have some inherent relevance to the story about to be performed.

When performing in schools or other educational settings, you may want to follow up your performance with activities that enable children to use the stories performed as a basis for extending their own learning. Performed stories can serve as the basis for children to read, write, or tell stories, create works of art, engage in scientific or mathematical exploration, or discuss some social issue raised during the performance. Performed stories can be tied to virtually every aspect of the school curriculum. For additional information involving the link between story performance and follow-up activity, consult the various texts provided in the Resources section of this chapter.

Sample Programs

To exemplify the previous comments, I have provided descriptions of two programs (see Examples 9.1 and 9.2) one lesson plan (see Example 9.3), and a unit plan (see Example 9.4) that I have performed in recent years. In the

Example 9.1

Program for Adults

Date: Oct. 29, 1998

Location: Atrium of the David Adamany Undergraduate Library, Wayne State University (Debbie Tucker, administrator)

Audience: University students & faculty; unpredictable number

Program Length: 45 minutes

Program Motif: Unusual People

Logistics:

Concern	Resolution
1. The atrium is an open area central to the library with much student/faculty traffic.	1. Have Debbie close off door to the south & put up detour signs so there won't be traffic behind me.
2. Two steps along the west wall form a stage; but no chairs will be provided in open area (faculty won't be comfortable on floor). Program to be videotaped.	2. Let audience sit on stage stairs. Put video camera behind audience on stage (can shoot over their heads). Perform from middle of atrium facing stage.
3. Video camera will be untended for much of the program.	3. Stay in one spot when performing; sit on a stool (have Debbie provide one).

Program:

Performance   Transition

1. Introduction: Recite "Invitation"
(Silverstein. *Where the Sidewalk
Ends*. Harper & Row, 1974, p. 9)

2. Tell "The Story of Mrs. Jones"
(O'Brien. *Mrs. Frisby & the Rats of
NIMH*. Atheneum, 1972, pp.
169–170)

                        That story is from Robert O'Brien's
                        Mrs. Frisby & the Rats of NIMH. (Show
book). Thanks for taking some time out
of your rat race today to listen to some
stories. All my stories today are about
unusual characters—appropriate with
Halloween approaching, a time when
we see all sorts of strange characters
about. But none more unique than
"the thief."

3. Tell "The Thief" (First heard a
version told by Dan Kedding; my
recreated version is set in pre-Colo-
nial Europe).

                        That story is set in the pre-colonial pe-
riod and could have been appreciated by
folks who had recently immigrated from
Europe. But other people living here
then were brought from Africa against
their wills. The slaves told stories too;
ones that demonstrated their unique in-
tellectual talents and the value of using
one's mind wisely. Let
me read you a short story about one
such unique person. The story is called
"The Knee-High Man" and this version
is taken from Diane Goode's *Book of
American Folk Tales & Songs* (1989,
Dutton pp. 19–21).

4. Read "The Knee-High Man."	It seems that justice was served in the two previous stories. But sometimes, to do the just thing involves very difficult decision making as will be seen in this next story.
5. Tell "Horseman in the Sky" (Adapted by R. Roney from Ambrose Bierce's original of the same name).	A print version of that story can be found in *Ambrose Bierce's Civil War* (William McCann [Ed.]. Washington, DC: Regnery Gateway, Inc., 1956, pp. 77–85) (Show book). Bierce's characters are haunting. Because we're so close to Halloween let me share another haunting tale with you. In Northville where I live there is a cemetery on Cady St. Back in the late 1800s one fall ...
6. Tell "The Dancing Skeleton."	Cynthia DeFelice has written a version of that story (Macmillan, 1989). (Show book). I'd like to leave you with another ghost story—perhaps the most celebrated ghost story in this country-about a truly unusual individual, the "Bell Witch." There are a number of sources for this story one of which is *The Bell Witch* by Sharon Shebar & Judith Schoder (Julian Messner, 1983).
7. Tell "The Bell Witch."	
8. Ending	I hope you've enjoyed the many unusual characters I've shared with you today and I hope you sleep soundly tonight.

Example 9.2

<u>Program for Primary Grade Children</u>

Date: March 22, 1985

Location: Conant Elementary School, Bloomfield Hills, MI
(Char Haun, Teacher Contact)

Audience: First & Second Grade Students (2 classes; @ 50
children)

Program Length: 30 minutes

Program Motif: None

Logistics:

<u>Concern</u>	<u>Resolution</u>
1. Children have been read to frequently. Limited exp. with storytelling.	1. Do a complete half hour program; mostly telling.
2. Children will be seated on carpet in one classroom.	2. Seating OK. Ask Char for a list of names of children; provide children with name tags pinned high on shirts or blouses. Be sure kids are comfortable on the floor & not bumping into one another.
3. Char will introduce me to children	3. Be prepared to clarify the "Dr." title.

Program:

Performance	Transition

1. Introduction:

a. Recite & invite finger play
participation:
"The hunters are creeping.
            Sshhhh!
The hunters are creeping.
            Sshhhh!
They don't make a sound
As their feet touch the
            ground.
The hunters are creeping.
            Sshhhh!"

(With right hand, walk two fingers
across left forearm held horizontally
for the "creeping" lines; bring index
finger to lips for "Sshhhh!" Invite
kids to copy my movement.)

b. (If introduced as Dr. Roney) Explain that I'm not the kind of
Dr. you go see if you're sick. I'm a story doctor and read lots of
books. Then the fun for me is to come to a school like Conant
Elementary and share what I've read with people like you.
Sometimes, I'll read from books and sometimes I'll just tell stories as I'm about to do. Are you comfortable? Is there enough
space between you & the people next to you so that you won't
accidentally bump someone with your elbow? OK.

2. Tell "The Little Boy's Secret."

That story comes from a book by David
Harrison (American Heritage Press,
1972) called *The Book of Giant Stories*.
(Show book) There are two other stories
in the book. One is about a giant who
throws temper tantrums. Have you ever
done that? The third story is about a giant who is afraid of butterflies. Are you
afraid of butterflies? Are cats or dogs
usually afraid of butterflies? What about
chicks & ducklings? Well my next story
is about a chick and duckling. Let's see
if they're afraid of butterflies or not.

This book is by Mirra Ginsburg. The illustrations are by Jose & Ariane Aruego.

3. Read aloud *The Chick & Duckling.* (Macmillan, 1972) (Invite children to "read" the predictable parts with you. Just nod to let them know it's OK to read along.)

Well, were the chick & duckling afraid of butterflies? Were they afraid of anything? Should they have been afraid of anything? Why? Why not? Well this next story is about some fradycats (or I should say, fradybears). Now I'd like you to help me tell this story just like you helped me read the last one. Divide the group in thirds and have each practice their part. (Group 1 says: "Eak, Creak, Squeak;" Group 2 says: "Tap, rap, snap." Group 3 says: "Bump, thump, clump.")

4. Tell *What Was That* (Golden Press, 1977)

Geda Mathews wrote the book and Normand Chartier illustrated it. (Show book) Those bears weren't very courageous but the person in our next story is. His name is Anansi. Now, Anansi was a very special person because ...

5. Tell *A Story A Story* (Atheneum, 1970)

If you liked that story, you can read it yourself. (Show book). It's written & illustrated by Gail Haley.

6. Ending:

Thank you for inviting me to share some stories with you. Mrs. Hahn told me that you haven't heard too many storytellers but you were great listeners this morning, so give yourselves a hand.

Example 9.3

<u>Lesson Plan for Kindergarten Children</u>

<u>I. Objective</u>	<u>II. Logistics</u>
1. Students will enjoy the lesson.	1. Enjoyment is engendered through teacher modeling (stories chosen & method of presentation are enjoyable to teacher).
2. Students' sense of story will be developed (written stories are the products of stories in one's head transmitted to print; stories follow a pattern).	2. Children create a new story, "Dinner," using the pattern original story "Lunch."
3. Students' improve ability to predict upcoming text.	3. Teacher informally encourages students to participate in the telling/reading of "Lunch."
4. Students improve ability to think analytically, synthetically, evaluatively.	4. Children analyze the art in the illustrated book, create a new text and illustrations for a book employing some techniques used by Fleming in *Lunch*.

<u>III. Program</u>

1. Teacher recites "Invitation" (Silverstein, *Where the Sidewalk Ends*, Harper, 1974).

2. Teacher tells "Great Big Enormous Turnip" using felt board.

3. Teacher tells "Lunch" using real vegetables/fruits (kept hidden in a bag & exposed partially to enable the children to guess each as story progresses):

        crisp white ... (turnip)

        tasty orange ... (carrots)

sweet yellow ... (corn)

tender green ... (peas)

tart blue ... (berries)

sour purple ... (grapes)

shinny red ... (apples)

juicy pink ... (watermelon)

4. Teacher reads *Lunch* (Fleming, Henry Holt & Co., 1992); encourages children to predict the name of the vegetables/ fruits.

Follow-up:

5. Children analyze illustrations in Lunch via teacher questioning:
    -How many mice are in the story?

    -How do you know that the mouse on this page is the same as the one on the next page? What does Mrs. Fleming do when drawing the mouse to let you know that it's the same mouse all the time? (Note the color: gray with pink nose & feet).

    -(Table leg page) What's this (point to table leg)? And this (point to table cloth)? So does Mrs. Fleming show you the whole table in this first picture?

    -(First turnip page) Does Mrs. Fleming show the whole turnip on this page? On the next page?

    -Does she show the whole carrot on this page? On the next page?

    -Does she show the whole ear of corn on this page? On the next page?

    -On later pages she'll show us some pea pods. On the first pea pod page, how much of the pea pod do you think she'll show us, part or whole? And on the second pea pod page? (Check the book to confirm children's responses).

    -Continue same line of questioning for grapes, apples, watermelon.

    -Have you been noticing the mouse? What's been happening to him?

6. Preparation for creating a new story in big book format through teacher questioning:

-Remember what the mouse ate? What are those things called? (Vegetables/fruits)

-How did the story end?

-At dinnertime, what do you suppose the mouse did then? And after he ate, what did he do then?

-And he would have slept until when? (Would there be any special event taking place the next morning that would be of special interest to a very hungry mouse?)

-Do you think that we could make up a new story about Mouse's adventures at dinnertime?

7. Creating a big book (see construction instructions below)

Display the big book (cover and sufficient pages for the number of children in the classroom have been constructed). Teacher questions:

-If Mrs. Fleming's story about Mouse's adventures at lunchtime is called "Lunch," what could we name our new story about his adventures at dinnertime?

-(Show *Lunch* book cover) Where on this big book cover should we put the title of our book?

-Mrs. Fleming put her name on the cover of her book because she's the author & illustrator. Who will be the author & illustrator of our book? Do we want to put our name on the cover? Where shall we put it? We won't have enough room to put each of our names on the cover, so how might we write our names all together as a group? (Teacher writes name on cover.)

-(Show first page of big book—to become the title page) Ask the title & author questions again (Teacher writes information on title page).

-(Show second page of big book) How should we start our story? (Show first text page of *Lunch*, if necessary.) (Teacher writes the dictated text: "Mouse was very hungry. He was so hungry,")

-What's the first thing he ate this time? What color was it? What kind of (green bean) was it? (Show *Lunch* text, if necessary) How did it taste? feel? (The intent is to get the children to create a noun phrase like "yummy green bean.") *Note the placement of the text on the pages: "He ate a yummy green" is placed on the front side of the page; "bean" is placed on the back side.*

-Continue questioning as in previous step up to the end of the story.

-(Ending) Well, we have to end our story. After Mouse ate, what did he do? (Show ending of *Lunch*, if necessary.) Elicit: "Then, he went to sleep until ... breakfast."

8. Illustrate the big book: Children in teams of two illustrate one page (front & back). Remind children how Mrs. Fleming illustrated her book; partial & whole pictures of vegetables/fruits. Instruct the pairs of children to talk & plan together before they begin drawing.

9. Put completed book together and read as a class.

Figure 9.1

Big Book Construction Instructions

Equipment:	Hole puncher Yard stick Large paper cutter Pencil Broad-tipped felt markers (at least two colors; be sure to have enough markers of the same dark color for the lettering)
Materials:	Metal loose-leaf rings (4 per book)—1½" diameter Posterboard (light colors only)—each book requires two boards cut to 19" × 25" (usually comes in 28" × 44" sheets) Manila oaktag—Purchase 18" × 24" sheets from an art supply store. Each book will require a varied number of sheets depending on the number of pages to be in the book (figure two children per page, front & back, including the front & back cover.)
Construction:	1. Using paper cutter, cut posterboard to size (2 pieces @19" × 25"); manila oaktag won't need cutting if purchased in 18" × 24" sheets. 2. Using hole puncher, cut four holes along one edge of posterboard. 3. Cut holes in second sheet of posterboard using first sheet as a guide. 4. Cut holes in *one sheet* of oaktag using one of the pre-punched posterboards as a guide. Position the oaktag flat against the posterboard, evenly spaced between the top to bottom of the board and with the edge of the oaktag flush with the edge of the posterboard. 5. Using this first sheet of oaktag as a guide, punch holes in the remaining sheets of oaktag.

Total cost of constructed big book—@ $8.

Example 9.4

A Storytelling Unit for Adolescents

Goals: To develop students' understanding of the human aspects
          of the Civil War and the implications for us today.

          To help students develop the ability to conduct historical
          research.

          To help students improve their ability to listen, speak, read,
          and write, and to think at higher levels.

Introduction to Unit: Display Civil War Artifacts Tell "A Cold Night"

          (Original: "A Cold Night" by Ambrose Bierce in Everett
          Bleiler (Ed.). *A Treasury of Victorian Ghost Stories*. New York:
          Charles Scribner's Sons, 1981, pp. 311–312)

Extension Activities:

1. Have students write for more information about the Battle of
Stones River:

    National Park Service Stones River National Battlefield

    Route 10, Box 495 Old Nashville Hwy.

    Murfreesboro, TN 37130

Be sure to request the publications sales list that provides titles and
prices for a variety of Civil War references including a map of the
troop movement during the battle, the video on the battle, artifacts
such as bullets, belt buckles and the monograph entitled *Tracing Your
Civil War Ancestor*.

2. Encourage students to locate a variety of resources describing the
Battle of Stones River and then compare the various versions. Contra-
dictory information is available regarding the following:

    -the significance of the battle

    -the winning side

    -the number of Confederate soldiers who fought in the battle

    -the number of Confederate casualties

    -the weather during the battle -the reasons for Gen. Bragg's deci-
    sion not to attack on Jan. 1, 1863

3. Map reading skill can be developed using troop movement maps of the battle. Can the students pinpoint the spot where the story, "A Cold Night," likely took place?

4. Have students create dioramas or drawings of the various stages of the battle (descriptions of the battle & troop movement maps can serve as a resource).

5. Have students create an illustrated alphabet book either on the Battle of Stones River ("a" for artillery, "b" for Braxton Bragg) or on the Civil War in general ("a" for Appomattox, "b" for Bull Run).

6. Encourage students to conduct a study of their own family history to discover if any of their ancestors were involved in the Civil War (Groene's text is helpful).

7. The Davis and Meltzer texts are full of brief stories. Students might select one to learn to tell. You might also encourage them to share ghost stories that they know or use the Bleiler text as a resource to learn one of the stories.

8. Using the Taper text, have students construct a letter responding to one of the entries. Have the students read selected letters in the text to note similarities and differences between today's writing styles and those prevalent during the Civil War.

9. Conduct discussions with small groups of students regarding the value (pro & con) of war, an issue raised in the story "A Cold Night."

10. Suggest students read other stories set in the Civil War including:

A Ballad of the Civil War, Mary Stolz (HarperCollins, 1997)
Behind Rebel Lines, Seymour Reit (Harcourt, 1988)
Bull Run, Paul Fleischman (HarperCollins, 1993)
Charlie Skedaddle, Patricia Beatty (Morrow, 1987)
Hew Against the Grain, Betty Sue Cummings (Atheneum, 1977)
The Killer Angels, Michael Shaara (Ballantine, 1974)
Nettie's Trip South, Ann Turner (Macmillan, 1987)
Pink and Say, Patricia Polacco (Philomel, 1994)

Shades of Gray, Carolyn Reeder (Macmillan, 1989)

Soldier's Heart , Gary Paulson (Delacorte, 1998)

Stonewall, Jean Fritz (Putnam, 1979)

The Tamarack Tree, Patricia Clapp (Lothrop, 1986)

Thunder at Gettysburg, Patricia Gauch (Putnam, 1990)

Turn Homeward, Hannalee, Patricia Beatty (Morrow, 1984)

With Every Drop of Blood, James & Christopher Collier (Delecorte, 1994)

The Yellow Bone Ring, Genevieve Gray (Lothrop, 1971)

Resources:

Bleiler, Everett (Ed.).(1981). *A treasury of Victorian ghost stories.* New York: Charles Scribner's Sons.

Catton, Bruce. (1960). *The American Heritage short history of the civil war.* New York: Dell Publishing Co.

Davis, Burke. (1982). *The civil war: Strange and Fascinating facts.* New York: The Fairfax Press.

Groene, Bertram. (1973). *Tracing your civil war ancestor.* Winston-Salem, NC: John F. Blair.

Meltzer, Milton. (1989). *Voices from the civil war.* New York: T. Y. Crowell.

Mitchell, Joseph. (1955). *Decisive battles of the civil war.* Greenwich, CT: Fawcett Publications.

Price, William. (1961). *Civil war handbook.* Fairfax, VA: Prince Lithography Co.

program for adults, it is important to note that this was the third in a series of performances over a 1-year period. The logistical concerns and resolutions stated here are the result of learning from the two previous performances. In the program for primary grade children, logistical concerns were dealt with via preliminary talks with the school contact. The lesson and unit plans are provided primarily to enable you to see how follow-up activities can be developed from a performance program.

DELIVERY

If you will be performing in a setting that is unfamiliar to you or you know that some logistical details need to be worked out on site, arrive well enough in advance of the performance to take care of these details. Check out the specific area in which you will perform and any equipment you will be using. Take the time to get comfortable with your surroundings. Immediately prior to the performance, arrange the audience to meet your programmatic needs if possible. In some settings, you may have no choice regarding the seating of your audience and will simply have to alter your performance to fit the situation. If something in the setting is a potential problem and can be altered, however, its best to do the changes beforehand. In classrooms, for example, I prefer to have the children sitting close by where I will be performing. This closeness is consistent with the intimacy that storytelling engenders and enables me to be in better control of my audience. If children are seated at desks, I'll usually ask if it is possible for them to be seated on the floor close by me during the performance. If this arrangement is impossible, then I know that I must inject more movement in my performance, which may mean substituting some stories for others to enable me to move more freely around the room.

As mentioned before, making eye contact with your audience is an important aspect of the story performance process. A corollary to eye contact involves learning to *read* your audience. If you are observant, you will know how an audience is reacting to the performance, which, in turn, will enable you to alter the performance to better meet their needs and suit their tastes. As a beginning performer, it is likely that most of your attention will be on the stories you are performing. But as you relax with a story over multiple performances, you'll want to begin to concentrate more and more on your audience. Interpreting the facial expressions, verbalizations, or body language of audience members is relatively easy. Attentiveness, pleasant looks, and comfortable body posture are indications that the story is going well. The opposite behavior may signal that your story (or some part of it) is confusing, inappropriate, too lengthy, or boring. Being able to read the reaction of your audience will enable you to make decisions on the spot about the performance—a vital skill to have as a performer.

Be prepared for unexpected behavior, particularly with young children, and know your story well so that you will be able to anticipate (and won't be surprised by) unusual reaction to some parts of your story. To the extent possible, try not to interrupt the flow of the performance; try to keep the flow going. Learn to ignore unusual behaviors that seem not to interrupt the concentration of your audience on the performance. For reactions that do break their concentration, try to work the reaction into the ongoing fabric of the story. In this way, you will pull the audience back into the story with a minimum of disruption. You must be able to think quickly in these instances, however. As such, it's a good idea to be fresh and rested when performing.

Fatigue may be the story performer's worst enemy beyond lack of adequate preparation. It interferes with your ability to concentrate on the story or the audience and can lead to disaster during a performance.

There are several things that you can do if you should draw a mental blank while telling stories. Ask your audience to remind you where you are in the story ("Now what have I told you so far in this story?"). Often their response will jog your memory. Sometimes its easiest to admit that you've lost the thread of the story and then start the story over again. (If you forget a second time, simply tell the audience that this story doesn't seem to want to be told today and go on to another one.) Plan for the possibility that you might forget sometime and have ready a comment such as, "You know folks, sometimes I do miss my mind. Now where were we in this story?" If you suddenly remember that you've left out a critical piece of a story, simply inject it into the story at that point in the telling by saying, "Now did I tell you that.... "

EXTENDED PRACTICE ACTIVITIES

Developmental Activities

1. Select five stories or poems you can perform and, using the guidelines in this chapter analyze the material for a common motif or theme. Then determine a sequence in which the material could be performed and develop transitions to link each of the stories as you might do in a program.

2. Search poetry books for potential introductions or endings to a story performance program. Create your own poem or ritual to begin and/or end a program.

3. Using the instructions from Fig. 9.1, construct a blank big book.

4. Keeping in mind a setting (e.g., classroom, local library, local recreation hall) with which you are familiar, identify any potential logistical concerns to be dealt with if you were to perform a program there. List potential solutions for each concern identified.

Culminating Activity

Plan a story performance program and then perform it for an appropriate audience.

RESOURCES

Barton, B., & Booth, D. (1990). *Stories in the classroom: Storytelling, reading aloud, and roleplaying with children.* Portsmouth, NH: Heinemann.

Britsch, B., & Dennison-Tansey, A. (1995). *One voice: Music and stories in the class-room*. Englewood, CO: Teacher Ideas Press.

Changar, J., & Harrison, A. (1992). *Storytelling activities kit: Ready-to-use techniques, lessons & listening cassettes for early childhood*. Oakland, CA: Center for Applied Research.

Collins, R., & Cooper, P. (1996). *The power of story: Teaching through storytelling*. Scottsdale, AZ: Gorsuch Scarisbrick Publishers.

Daily, S. (Ed.). (1994). *Tales as tools: The power of storytelling in the classroom*. Jonesborough, TN: National Storytelling Association.

Denman, G. (1991). *Sit tight & I'll swing you a tale: Using & writing stories with young people*. Portsmouth, NH: Heinemann.

Ellis, B. (1997). *Learning from the land: Teaching ecology through stories & activities*. Englewood, CO: Teacher Ideas Press.

Gillard, M. (1995). *Storyteller, storyteacher: Discovering the power of storytelling for teaching & living*. York, ME: Stenhouse Publications.

Hamilton, M., & Weiss, M. (1990). *Children tell stories: A teaching guide*. Katonah, NY: Richard C. Owen Publishers.

King, N. (1993). *Storymaking & drama: An approach to teaching language & literature at the secondary & postsecondary levels*. Portsmouth, NH: Heinemann.

Lipke, B. (1996). *Storytelling in mathematics & science*. Portsmouth, NH: Heinemann.

Livo, N., & Reitz, S. (1987). *Storytelling activities*. Littleton, CO: Libraries Unlimited.

Marsh, V., & Luzadder, P. (1986). *Story puzzles: Tales in the tangram tradition*. Fort Atkinson, WI: Highsmith Press.

Miller, T., & Pellowski, A. (1988). *Joining in: An anthology of audience participation stories & how to tell them*. Cambridge, MA: Yellow Moon Press.

Roney, R. C. (1993). Telling stories: A key to reading and writing. In G. Blatt (Ed.), *Once upon a folklore: Capturing the folklore process with children* (pp. 9–23). New York: Teacher's College Press.

Rubright, L. (1996). *Beyond the beanstalk: Interdisciplinary learning through storytelling*. Portsmouth, NH: Heinemann.

Weaver, M. (Ed.). (1995). *Many voices: True tales from America's past*. Jonesborough, TN: National Storytelling Association.

References

Allen, P. (1982). *Who sank the boat?* New York: Coward McCann.

Amato, A., Emans, R., & Ziegler, E. (1973). The effects of creative dramatics and storytelling in a library setting. *The Journal of Educational Research, 67*(4), 161–165.

Andrews, J. (1985). *Very last first time.* Vancouver: Douglas & McIntyre.

Bailey, G. (1970). *The use of a library resource program for improvement of language abilities of disadvantaged first grade pupils.* Unpublished doctoral dissertation, Boston College, Boston, MA.

Balian, L. (1994a). *The aminal.* Watertown, WI: Humbug Books.

Balian, L. (1994b). *Humbug witch.* Watertown, WI: Humbug Books.

Balian, L. (1997). *Humbug rabbit.* Watertown, WI: Humbug Books.

Barton, B. (1995). *Tools.* New York: HarperCollins.

Bode, J., & Mack, S. (1996). *Hard time: A real life look at juvenile crime and violence.* New York: Delacorte.

Briggs, R. (1970). *Jim and the beanstalk.* New York: Coward, McCann & Geoghegan.

Briggs, R. (1978). *The snowman.* New York: Random House.

Brown, M. (1954). *Cinderella.* New York: Charles Scribner's Sons.

Brown M. (1961). *Once a mouse....* New York: Charles Scribner's Sons.

Burningham, J. (1970). *Mr. Gumpy's outing.* New York: Holt, Rinehart & Winston.

Burroughs, M. (1970). *The stimulation of verbal behavior in culturally disadvantaged three-year-olds.* Unpublished doctoral dissertation, Michigan State University, East Lansing, MI.

Butler, D. (1980). *Cushla and her books.* Boston, MA: The Horn Book.

Campbell, D., & Campbell, T. (1976, April). *Psychology in the Schools, 13*(2), 201–204.

Carle, E. (1971). *Do you want to be my friend?* New York: Thomas Y. Crowell.

Cazden, C. (1965). *Environmental assistance to the child's acquisition of grammar.* Unpublished doctoral dissertation, Harvard University, Boston, MA.

Chomsky, C. (1972, February). Stages of language development and reading exposure. *Harvard Educational Review, 42,* 1–33.

Clark, M. (1976). *Young fluent readers.* London: Heinemann Educational Books.

Clay, M. (1979). *Stones: The concepts about print test.* Portsmouth, NH: Heinemann.

Cleary, B. (1984). *Ramona forever.* New York: William Morrow.

Coatsworth, E. (1930). *The cat who went to heaven.* New York: Macmillan.

Cohen, D. (1968, February). The effect of literature on vocabulary and reading achievement. *Elementary English, 45,* 209–213, 217.

Cooney, C. B. (1997). *The terrorist.* New York: Scholastic.

Cowen-Fletcher, J. (1993). *Mama zooms.* New York: Scholastic.

Cullinan, B. (1974, January). Language expansion for black children in the primary grades: A research report. *Young Children, 29,* 98–112.

Cushman, K. (1995). *The midwife's apprentice.* New York: Clarion.

Davis, D. (1993). *Telling your own stories.* Little Rock, AR: August House.

Demi. (1998). *The greatest treasure.* New York: Scholastic.

Dennis, I. (Ed.). (1967). *New comic limericks.* Kansas City, MO: Hallmark Cards.

de Paola, T. (1978a). *Bill and Pete.* New York: G. P. Putnam's Sons.

dePaola, T. (1978b). *Pancakes for breakfast.* New York: Harcourt Brace Jovanovich.

DiSalvo-Ryan, D. (1991). *Uncle Willie and the soup kitchen.* New York: William Morrow & Co., Inc.

Dixon, K. (1992, Winter/Spring). Storytelling World presents: Donald Davis. *Storytelling World, 1*(1), 7–10.

Domanska, J. (1969). *The turnip.* New York: Collier.

Doss, P. (1982). *Emotional expressions of eleven- and twelve-year-old children as seen through their creative arts during a school year.* Unpublished doctoral dissertation, Pacific Graduate School of Psychology, Palo Alto, CA.

Druce, A. (1993). *Chalk talk stories.* Lanham, MD: Scarecrow.

Durkin, D. (1966). *Children who read early.* New York: Columbia Teachers College Press.

Farrell, C., & Nessel, D. (1982). *Effects of storytelling: An ancient art for modern classrooms.* San Francisco, CA: The Zellerbach Family Fund.

Feitelson, D., Kita, B., & Goldstein, Z. (1986). Effects of listening to series stories on first graders' comprehension and use of language. *Research in the Teaching of English, 20*(4), 339–356.

Ferris, H. (Ed.). (1957). *Poems old and new.* New York: Doubleday.

Fisher, C, & Natarella, M. (December, 1982). Young children's preferences in poetry: A national survey of first, second, and third graders. *Research in the Teaching of English, 16,* 339–354.

Fleming, D. (1992). *Lunch.* New York: Henry Holt.

Fodor, M. (1966). *The effect of systematic reading of stories on the language development of culturally deprived children.* Unpublished doctoral dissertation, Cornell University, Ithaca, NY.

Freeman, D. (1964). *Dandelion.* New York: Viking Press.

Froyen, G. E. (1987). *The effects of storytelling experiences on vocabulary skills of second grade students.* Unpublished master's thesis, University of Northern Iowa, Cedar Falls, IA.

Galda, L., & Cullinan, B. (1991). Literature for literacy: What research says about the benefits of using trade books in the classroom. In J. Flood, J. M. Jensen, D. Lapp, & J. R. Squire (Eds.), *Handbook of research on teaching the English language arts* (pp. 529–535). New York: Macmillan.

Galdone, P. (1973). *The three billy goats gruff.* New York: Seabury Press.

Ginsburg, M. (1972). *The chick and the duckling.* New York: Macmillan.

Ginsburg, M. (1982). *The sun's asleep behind the hill.* New York: Greenwillow.

Goodall, J. S. (1987). *The story of a main street.* New York: Macmillan.

Grimes, N. (1978). *Something on my mind.* New York: Dial Books For Young Readers.

Hamilton, V. (1985). "The people could fly." in V. Hamilton (Ed.), *The people could fly: American Black folktales* (pp. 166–173). New York: Alfred A. Knopf.

Hansen, H. (1969, January). The impact of the home literacy environment on reading attitude. *Elementary English, 46,* 17–24.

Hansen, H. (1973, January). The home literacy environment—a follow-up report. *Elementary English, 50,* 97–98, 122.

Hobbs, W., & Kastner, J. (1997). *Beardance.* New York: Atheneum Books for Young Readers.

Huck, C., Hepler, S., Hickman, J., & Kiefer, B. (1997). *Children's literature in the elementary school.* Madison, WI: Brown & Benchmark.

Hutchins, P. (1983). *Rosie's walk.* New York: Macmillan.

Irwin, O. C. (1960, June). Infant speech: Effect of systematic reading of stories. *Journal of Speech and Hearing Research, 3,* 187–190.

Jonas, A. (1989). *Color dance.* New York: Greenwillow.

Joy, F. (1981). *Shadow characters for storytelling.* Johnson City, TN: Kreative Konnections Publication.

Joy, F. (Ed.). (1992, Summer/Fall). A special issue about historytelling. *Storytelling World, 1*(2).

Joy, F. (Ed.). (1993, Summer/Fall). Tickling tales. *Storytelling World, 2*(2).

Joy, F. (Ed.). (1994, Summer/Fall). Multicultural storytelling. *Storytelling World, 3*(2).

Joy, F. (Ed.). (1997, Winter/Spring). Creating and crafting stories. *Storytelling World, Issue 11.*

Kennedy, R. (1979). *Inside my feet.* New York: HarperCollins.

Kevin, J. (1996, Summer/Fall). Copyright issues for storytellers. *Storytelling World, Issue 10.*

Kipling, R. (1952). *Just so stories* Garden City, NY: Doubleday.

Klein, S. (1999, Winter/Spring). Ethics, apprenticeship, etiquette, courtesy, and copyright. *Storytelling World, 15,* 2–13.

Kraus, R. (1970). *Whose mouse are you?* New York: Macmillan.

Kutiper, K. S. (1985). *A survey of the adolescent poetry preferences of seventh, eighth, and ninth graders.* Unpublished doctoral dissertation, University of Houston, TX.

Levine, G. C. (1997). *Ella enchanted.* New York: HarperCollins.

Lionni, L. (1959). *Little blue and little yellow.* New York: Ivan Obolensky.

Lionni, L. (1960). *Inch by inch.* New York: AstorHonor.

Lionni, L. (1969). *Alexander and the wind-up mouse.* New York: Random House.

Livo, N. (1983, September). Turkish storyteller's poem. *Media & Methods, 25.*

Marsh, V. (1992). *Paper cutting stories from a to z.* Fort Atkinson, WI: Highsmith.

Marsh, V. (1994). *Paper cutting stories for holidays & special events.* Fort Atkinson, WI: Highsmith.

Martin, B., Jr., & Archambault, J. (1986). *White Dynamite and Curly Kidd.* New York: Holt, Rinehart & Winston.

Martin, R., & Gammell, S. (1989). *Will's mammoth.* New York: G. P. Putnam's Sons.

Mathis, S. B. (1975). *The hundred penny box.* New York: Viking Press.

McCormick, S. (1977, February). Should you read aloud to your children? *Language Arts, 54,* 139–143.

McDermott, G. (1975). *The stonecutter: A Japanese folk tale.* New York: Viking Press.

McDermott, G. (1980). *Sun flight.* New York: Four Winds Press.

McKissack, P. (1986). *Flossie and the fox.* New York: Dial.

Mendez, P., & Byard, C. (1989). *The black snowman.* New York: Scholastic.

Milhous, K., & Dalgliesh, A. (1990). *The turnip.* New York: Philomel.

Moffett, J. (1983). *Teaching the universe of discourse.* Boston, MA: Houghton Mifflin.

Newton, P. (1990). *The stonecutter.* New York: G. P. Putnam's Sons.

Nilsen, A. (1995). *Literature for today's young adults.* New York: HarperCollins.

Ninio, A., & Bruner, J. (1973). The achievement and antecedents of labelling. *Journal of Child Language, 5,* 1–15.

Nones, E. (1989). *Wendell.* New York: Farrar, Straus, & Giroux.

Nones, E. (1995). *Angela's wings.* New York: Farrar, Straus, & Giroux.

Norton, D. (1999). *Through the eyes of a child: An introduction to children's literature.* Englewood Cliffs, NJ: Prentice-Hall.

O'Brien, R. (1972). *Mrs. Frisby and the rats of NIMH.* New York: Atheneum.

Orwell, G. (1954). *Animal farm.* New York: Harcourt Brace Jovanovich.

Painter, W. (1990). *Storyhours with puppets and other props.* North Haven, CT: Shoe String Press.

Pellowski, A. (1984). *The story vine: A source book of unusual and easy-to-tell stories from around the world.* New York: Macmillan.

Peng, M. (1989). *Conflicting emotions: Elicited understanding in younger children.* Unpublished doctoral dissertation, University of Pittsburgh, Pittsburgh, PA.

Peter Pauper Press. (1954). *Peter Pauper's limerick book.* Mount Vernon, NY: Author.

Petersen, R. (1995, Winter/Spring). Story sounds. *Storytelling World, 4*(1).

Philpot, J. (1994a). *Scissor-tales for any day: Storytelling cutups, activities & extensions.* Nashville, TN: Incentive Publications.

Philpot, J. (1994b). *Scissor-tales for special days: Storytelling cutups, activities & extensions.* Nashville, TN: Incentive Publications.

Polacco, P. (1994). *Pink and Say.* New York: Philomel Books.

Porter, E. J. (1971, March). Project promise, recruiting high school students for teaching in city schools. *Elementary English, 48*, 336–340.

Provenzo, E. F., Provenzo, A. B., & Zorn, P. A. (1984). *Pursuing the past: Oral history, photographs, family history, cemeteries.* Menlo Park, CA: Addison-Wesley.

Robinson, B. (1972). *The best Christmas pageant ever.* New York: Harper & Row.

Rockwell, T. (1973). *How to eat fried worms.* New York: Franklin Watts.

Roffey, M. (1982). *Home sweet home.* New York: Coward-McCann.

Rohmann, E. (1994). *Time flies.* New York: Crown.

Roney, R. C. (1975). *The effects of two promotional teaching techniques on the amount of personal reading and selection of books by fourth grade children.* Unpublished doctoral dissertation, University of Colorado, Boulder, CO.

Roney, R. C. (1980, Winter). Reading aloud to children—why bother? *Michigan Reading Journal, 14*(1), 36–38.

Roney, R. C. (1984, November). Background experience is the foundation of success in learning to read. *The Reading Teacher, 38*, 196–199.

Roney, R. C. (1986). Research report being prepared for publication.

Roney, R. C. (1989, March). Back to the basics with storytelling. *The Reading Teacher, 42*, 520–523.

Roney, R. C. (1993). Telling stories: A key to reading and writing. In G. T. Blatt (Ed.), *Once upon a folktale: Capturing the folklore process with children* (pp. 9–23). New York: Teachers College Press.

Roney, R. C. (1998, Winter/Spring). Defining storytelling: Some theoretical thoughts. *Storytelling World, 13*, 23.

Ross-Albers, S. (Fall, 1989). *Using shadow puppetry to dramatize children's literature.* Unpublished master's project, Wayne State University, Detroit, MI.

Salus, N. (1979). *My daddy's mustache.* Garden City, NY: Doubleday.

Sattler, H. (1985). *Train whistles.* New York: Lothrop, Lee & Shepard Books.

Sebesta, S. (1983). Choosing poetry. In N. Roser & M. Frith (Eds.), *Children's choices* (pp. 66–78). Newark, DE: International Reading Association.

Sendak, M. (1962). *Pierre.* New York: Harper & Row.

Sendak, M. (1963). *Where the wild things are.* New York: Harper & Row.

Shannon, G. (1981). *Lizard's song.* New York: Greenwillow.

Shannon, G. (1983). *The surprise.* New York: Greenwillow.

Sharmat, M. (1980). *Gregory, the terrible eater.* New York: Four Winds Press.

Short, K. (Ed.). (1995). *Research and professional resources in children's literature: Piecing a patchwork quilt.* Newark DE: International Reading Association.

Silverstein, S. (1974). *Where the sidewalk ends.* New York: Harper & Row.

Silverstein, S. (1996). *Falling up.* New York: HarperCollins.

Sirota, B. (1971). *The effect of a planned literature program of daily oral reading by the teacher on the voluntary reading of fifth grade children.* Unpublished doctoral dissertation, New York University, New York.

Small, D. (1994). *George Washington's cows.* New York: Farrar, Straus, & Giroux.

Sostarich, J. (1974). *A study of the reading behavior of sixth graders: Comparisons of active and other readers.* Unpublished doctoral dissertation, Ohio State University, Columbus, OH.

Speare, E. G. (1983). *The sign of the beaver.* Boston: Houghton Mifflin.

Staples, S. F. (1996). *Dangerous skies.* New York: Farrar, Straus, & Giroux.

Steig, W. (1971). *Amos and Boris.* New York: Farrar, Straus, & Giroux.

Taback, S. (1998). *There was an old lady who swallowed a fly.* New York: Viking Press.

Terry, A. (1974). *Children's poetry preferences: A national survey of upper elementary grades.* Urbana, IL: National Council of Teachers of English.

Thayer, E., & Polacco, P. (1988). *Casey at the bat.* New York: G. P. Putnam's Sons.

Thorndike, R. (1973). *Reading comprehension, education in 15 countries: An empirical study* (Vol. 3.). New York: Holstead Wiley.

Tison, A., & Taylor, T. (1971). *The adventures of the three colors.* New York: World Publishing.

Turkle, B. (1976). *Deep in the forest.* New York: E. P. Dutton.

Van Allsburg, C. (1982). *Ben's dream.* Boston, MA: Houghton Mifflin.

Van Allsburg, C. (1990). *Just a dream.* New York: Scholastic.

Van Allsburg, C. (1991). *Tuesday.* New York: Clarion.

Ward, L. (1973). *The silver pony.* Boston, MA: Houghton Mifflin.

Welch, W. (1995). *Playing right field.* New York: Scholastic.

Wells, G. (1986). *The meaning makers.* Portsmouth, NH: Heinemann.

White, E. B. (1952). *Charlotte's web.* Harper & Row.

Wiesner, David. (1991). *Tuesday.* New York: Clarion.

Williams, B. (1974). *Albert's toothache.* New York: E. P. Dutton.

Williams, J. (1973). *Petronella.* New York: Parents Magazine Press.

Wolkstein, D. (1996). *The magic orange tree and other Haitian folktales.* New York: Schocken Books.

Wood, A., & Wood, D. (1984). *The napping house.* San Diego, CA: Harcourt Brace Jovanovich.

Yashima, T. (1955). *Crow Boy.* New York: Viking Press.

Yolen, J. (1987a). *Owl moon.* New York: Philomel.

Yolen, J. (1987b). *Piggins.* San Diego: Harcourt Brace Jovanovich.

Young, Y. (1988). *The effects of storytelling on children's listening skills.* Unpublished master's thesis, University of Oregon, Eugene, OR.

Zeitlin, S. J., Kotkin, A. J., & Baker, H. C. (1982). *A celebration of American family folklore.* New York: Pantheon.

Zemach, M., & Zemach, H. (1966). *The fisherman and his wife.* New York: W. W. Norton.

Zemach, M., & Zemach, H. (1976). *It could always be worse.* New York: Farrar, Straus, & Giroux.

Author Index

Subject Index

About the Author

Dr. R. Craig Roney, an Associate Professor of Teacher Education at Wayne State University in Detroit, specializes in children's literature, storytelling, and language arts education. He has been teaching adults to tell stories for over 20 years. His experience combined with his research involving teaching storytelling to adults serves as the theoretical and practical basis for this text.